REFRIGERATION AND AIR CONDITION TECHNICIAN SECOND YEAR MCQ

REFRIGERATION AND AIR CONDITION TECHNICIAN SECOND YEAR MCQ

MANOJ DOLE

Digitization is the need of the time. In the future, training in industrial training institutes will need to be conducted using online internet to make training more convenient and easy. E-books containing a set of MCQ questions will be made available to the trainees as they need to be more accustomed to the multiple choice questions MCQ to prepare for the online exams taking place in their industrial training institutes.

With all these factors in mind, Mr. Manoj Madhukar Dole Instructor, Industrial Training Institute, Satara, has written books according to the new annual system and NSQF-5 syllabus. And they've created theoretical mobile apps and blogs to make training easier, and made all these educational materials available for download on the world famous websites Google Play Store, Amazon and Apple Book Store.

The books were published by Hon'ble Joint Director Shri Rajendra Ghume Saheb Regional Office of Vocational Education and Training, Pune on 9/1/2019, at this time Shri Prakash Saigavkar Saheb Principal Government Industrial Training Institute Aundh Pune, Shri Tukaram Misal Saheb Principal Govt. Q. Sanstha Satara, Shri Sachin Dhumal Saheb District Vocational Education and Training Officer Satara, Shri Yatin Pargaonkar Saheb Principal Govt. Q. Sanstha Kolhapur, Shri Vikas Teke Saheb Inspector Vocational Education and Training Regional Office Pune, Palekar Foods Products Pvt. Ltd. Entrepreneurial Chairman of Satara Mr. Nilkanthrao Palekar Saheb, Chairman of Hira Foods Mr. Ibrahim Baba Tamboli Saheb, Mrs. Shalmali Pawar Headmaster Government Technical School Center Satara and other dignitaries were present on the occasion.

Contents

Prologue

Refrigeration and Air Condition Technician Second Year MCQ is a simple Book for ITI Course Revised NSQ F-5 Syllabus, It contains objective questions with underlined & bold correct answers MCQ covering all topics including all about the latest & Important about Carry out servicing, dismantling, checking different parts of different types of commercial compressor, re-placing worn out parts, Check lubrication system. Assemble & check performance. Perform servicing of different types of water-cooled condenser. Perform servicing and performance test of Cooling tower Conduct Servicing, backwash & re-generate Water treatment plant of circulating water. Perform Fitting of expansion valve, adjustment of refrigerant flow according to heat load. Perform servicing of evaporator & chillers. Carry out servicing and retrofit of Water cooler and dispenser. Service, retrofit of visible cooler and bottle cooler and test performance. Conduct servicing of deep freezer and test performance. Install, service, repair, gas charging and testing performance of Ice Cube machine. Repair, servicing & retrofit of ice candy plant. Perform servicing of Ice plant and evaporative condenser. Perform Servicing and preventive maintenance of walk in cooler & cold storage. Study psychrometric chart and measure psychrometric properties using psychrometric, anemometer i.e. DBT, WBT, RH, air flow etc. Perform servicing of motor and blowers used in different air conditioning system. Construct, install, pack thermal and acoustic insulation of different air ducts. Perform servicing and maintenance of different types of air filters. Perform servicing, installation, fault diagnosis and remedial measures on Package AC with Air cooled condenser.

We add new question answers with each new version. Please email us in case of any errors/omissions. This is arguably the largest and best e-Book for All engineering multiple choice questions and answers.

As a student you can use it for your exam prep. This e-Book is also useful for professors to refresh material.

Foreword

Vocational education and training is imparted through the Department of Vocational Education and Training through the Department of Business Education and Business Practical to supply multi-skilled artisans in line with the rapidly growing demand in the industrial sector in the 21st century. All the occupations within the institutions are important, as the trainees from these occupations develop multi-skills as per the demands of the industry.

with the noble intention of making available MCQ e-books suitable for all businesses, considering that all the examinations in all the industries in the industrial sector are conducted online and include MCQ method questions. Mr. Manoj Madhukar Dole has written a very good e-book on MCQ method as per the new annual syllabus. This e-book will definitely be a guide for all the trainees, trainee candidates, training instructors and others concerned.

The author of the book is Mr. Manoj Madhukar Dole, Instructor Gov. ITI Satara has 17 years of training experience. Written as a new annual pattern, this e-book incorporates modern digital QR Code technology to understand the layout, simple language, and simple syntax, diagrams and videos for each subject. So I am sure that this e-book will definitely be useful for in-depth study and exam practice. The work they have done is certainly commendable.

Mr. Tukaram Misal
Principal Government Industrial Training Institute Satara.

Preface

DGET New Delhi and CSTARI Kolkata have been implementing an annual pattern for all businesses in ITI since the August 2018 session. The examination system will also be changed and it will be online from this year and since all the questions are of Objective Type (MCQ), the trainees are in dire need of in-depth study. It is with this in mind that we are delighted to present the books based on the old NIMI pattern and a complete overview of the new annual pattern, and we hope that these books will be a guide for all business directors and trainees. Is.

For writing these books, Johar Awate Saheb, Principal of ITI Akluj. Former Principal of ITI Satara Saigavkar Saheb, Assistant Director Shri Chandrakant Dhekne Saheb Regional Office of Vocational Education and Training, Pune, District Vocational Education and Training Officer Sachin Dhumal Saheb and Headmaster Government Technical School Kendra Shalmali Pawar Madam and son Adhiraj Dole, mother Kusum Dole, I am very grateful to my father Madhukar Dole and wife Ashwini Dole for their special guidance and cooperation from time to time.

Also, in a very short period of time, the book was reviewed by Shri Rajendra Ghume Saheb, Joint Director, Vocational Education and Training Regional Office, Pune, for his invaluable time in publishing the book. I am sincerely grateful for their feedback.

I am grateful to the Instructor of ITI Satara for there continuous support from the very beginning of writing the book.

From this book, I consider myself blessed to have shared my thoughts on e-learning with you. I will not claim that this book is perfect, because considering the perfection, this book is an attempt and is in its infancy. They will be valuable for improvement if they are tested and suggested.

Manoj Dole
Dated 9/1/2019

Acknowledgements

The industrial training and theoretical examination system of our industrial training institutes and these changes have been accepted by the craft instructors and the trainees. Theoretical examinations conducted in your industrial training institutes are also conducted online. Since these examinations are of multiple choice MCQ method, the trainees will need to get more practice of such questions.

With all these considerations in mind, Mr. Manoj Madhukar, Director, Dole Crafts, Katari Industrial Training Institute, Satara, has done a thorough study and with his diligent work and added his keen intellect, according to the new annual system and NSQF-5 syllabus, e-book of Katari and other machine trades. -Book) and they have created mobile apps and blogs on theoretical topics to make training easier and have made all these educational materials available for download on the world famous websites Google Play Store, Amazon and Apple Book Store. Training has been made easier by creating a print version and using advanced techniques like QR Code.

All these educational materials will definitely be a guide for all the trainees for in-depth study and for the craft instructors and other concerned who are imparting vocational training.

CHAPTER ONE

Refrigeration and Air Condition Technician Second Year MCQ Drawing

Online Test Exam
ITI Books
CNC Course
AutoCAD CAM
JOB & Apprentice
Online Theory
Computer Course
Trading Course
Web Designing
MSCIT Course
Shopping Business
Internet Business
Remotasks Course
Online Services
Top Sportsmans
Indian Army
Freedom Fighters
Top Scientists
Social Reformers
Motivational Speaker
Top Richest People
Join WhatsApp Group
Join Facebook Group
Like Facebook Page
PAN / Adhar / Licence Passport

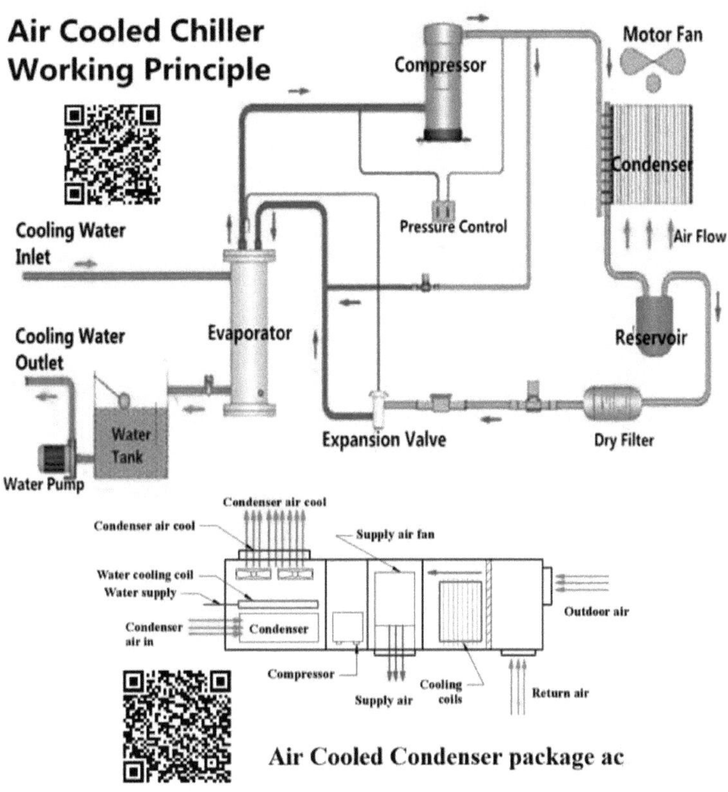

Air Cooled Condenser package ac

WATER COOLER PARTS IDENTIFICATION

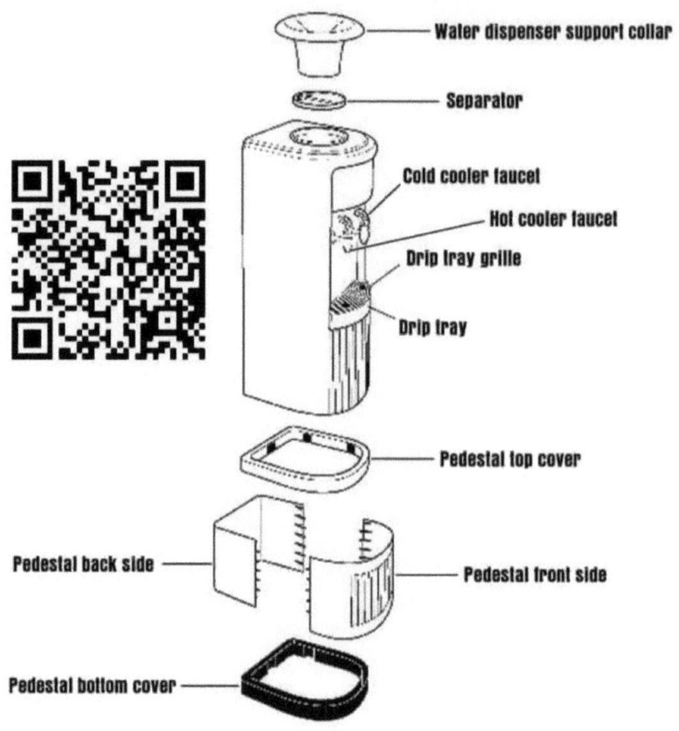

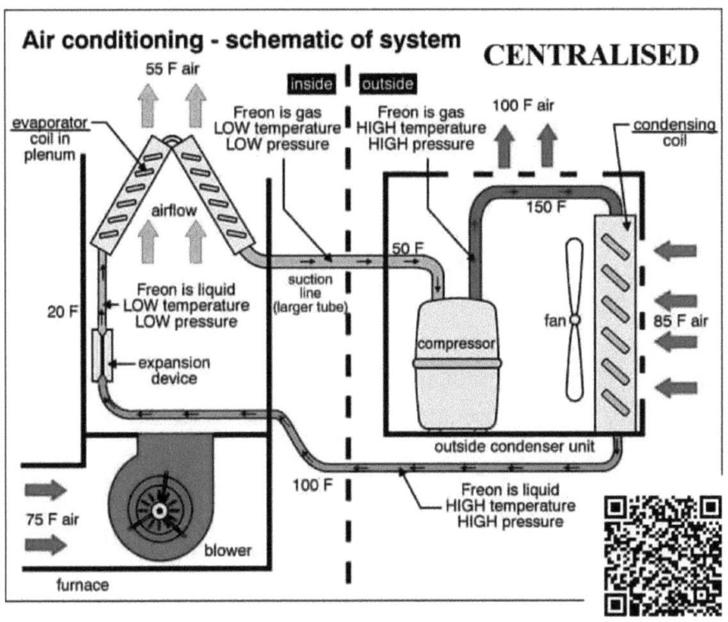
Air conditioning - schematic of system
CENTRALISED
55 F air
inside
outside
evaporator coil in plenum
Freon is gas
LOW temperature
LOW pressure
Freon is gas
HIGH temperature
HIGH pressure
100 F air
condensing coil
airflow
150 F
50 F
suction line (larger tube)
Freon is liquid
LOW temperature
LOW pressure
20 F
compressor
fan
85 F air
expansion device
outside condenser unit
100 F
Freon is liquid
HIGH temperature
HIGH pressure
75 F air
blower
furnace

COLD STORAGE

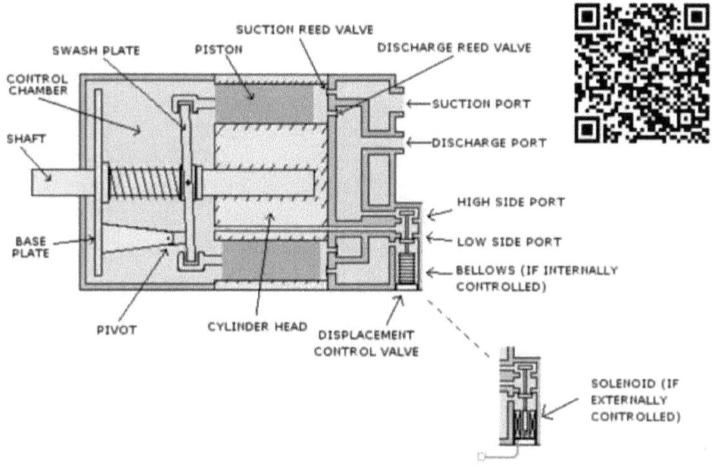

INTERNAL STRUCTURE OF VARIABLE DISPLACEMENT COMPRESSOR

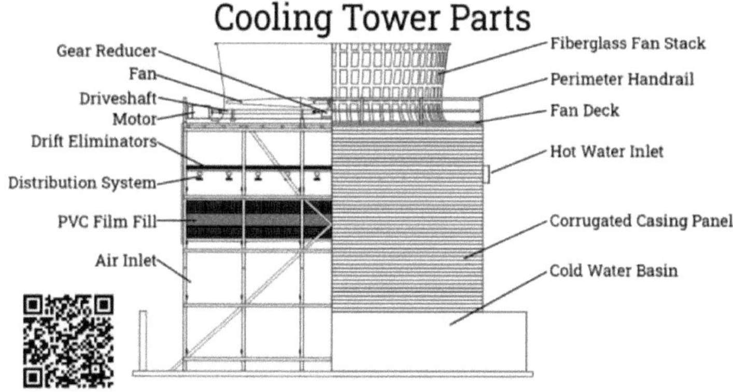

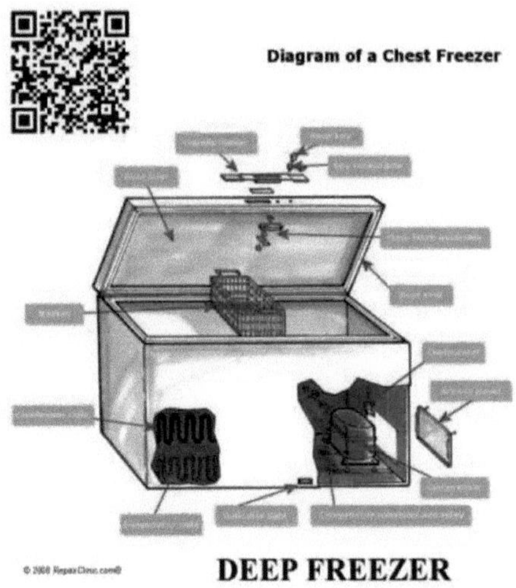

DEEP FREEZER

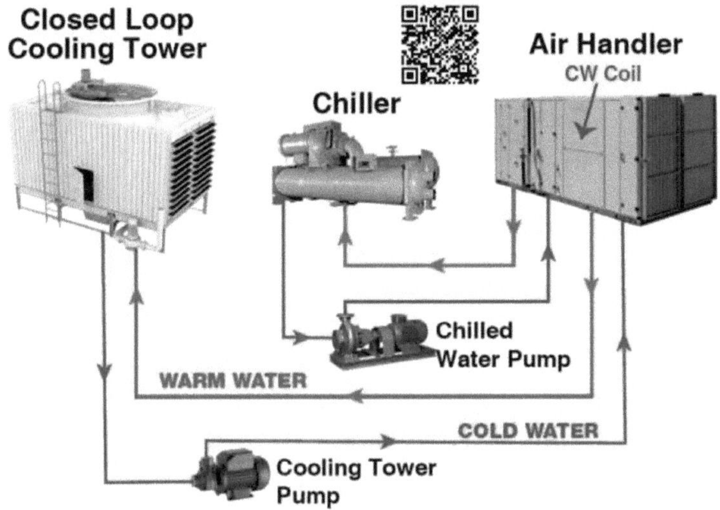
DIRECT SYSTEM
Closed Loop
Cooling Tower
Air Handler
CW Coil
Chiller
Chilled
Water Pump
WARM WATER
COLD WATER
Cooling Tower
Pump

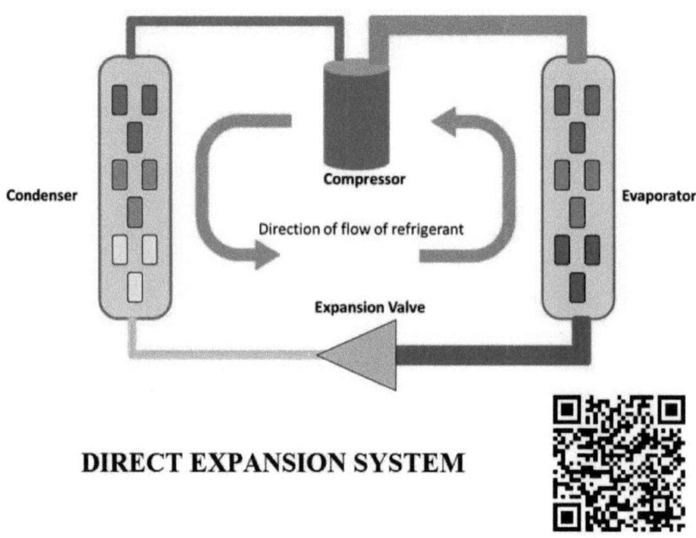

DIRECT EXPANSION SYSTEM

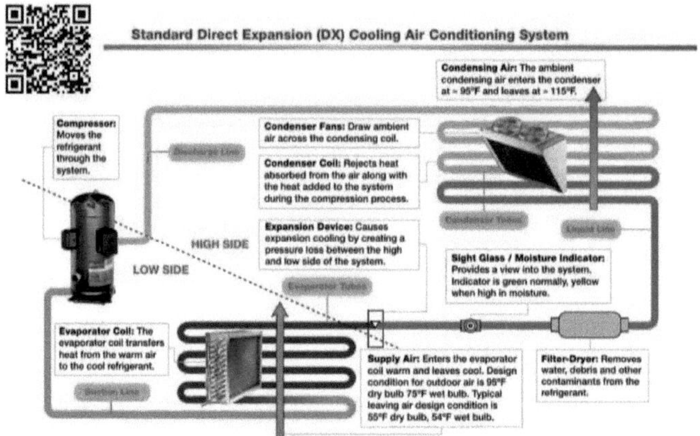

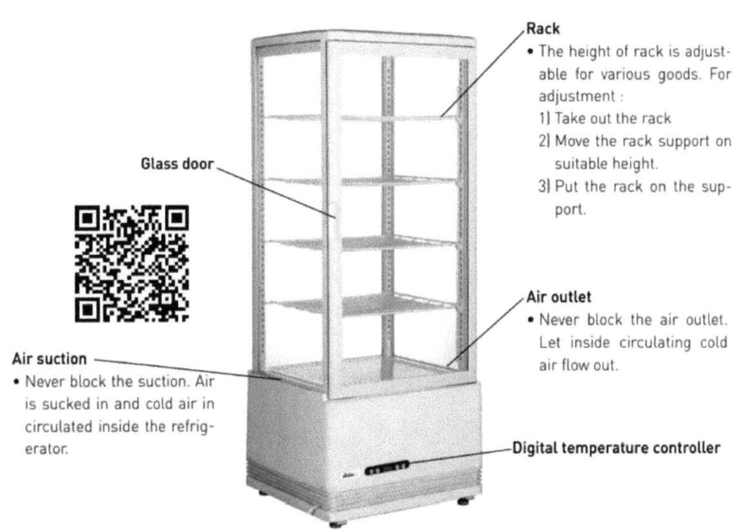

DISPLAY CABINET

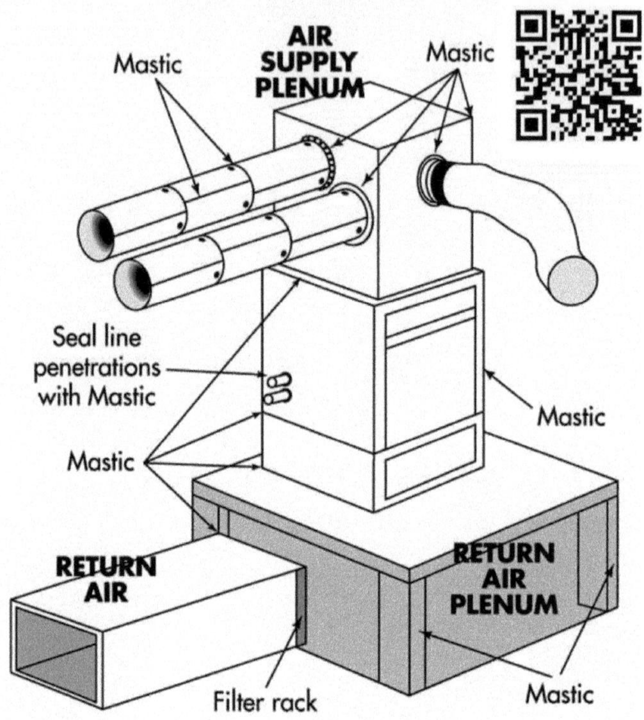
Air Handler DUCT
AIR
SUPPLY
PLENUM
Mastic
Mastic
Seal line
penetrations
with Mastic
Mastic
Mastic
RETURN
AIR
RETURN
AIR
PLENUM
Filter rack
Mastic

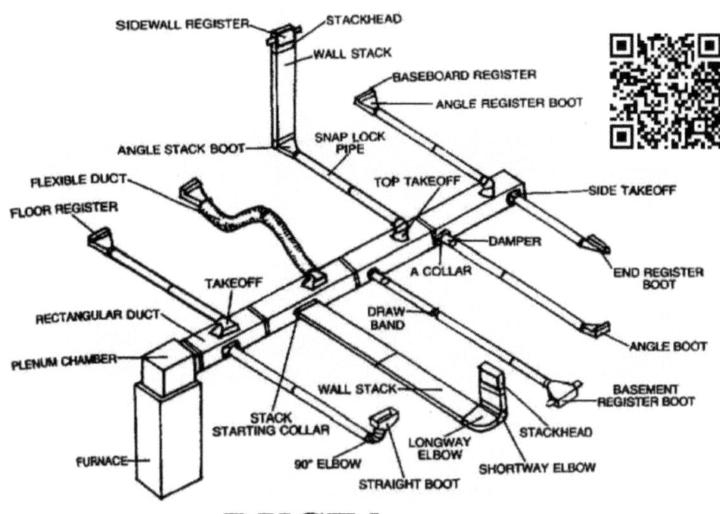

DUCT layout

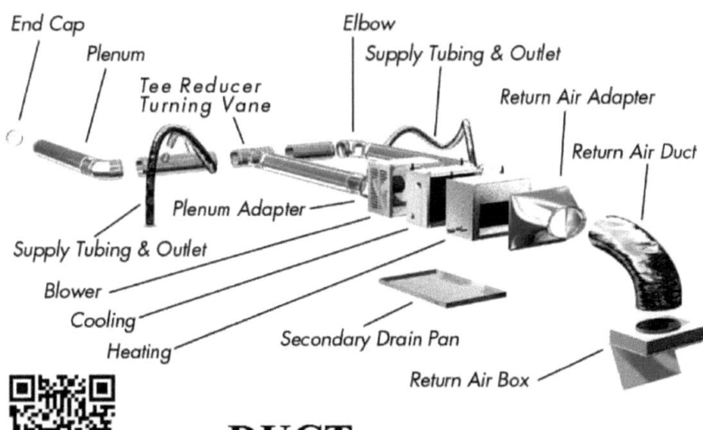

DUCT

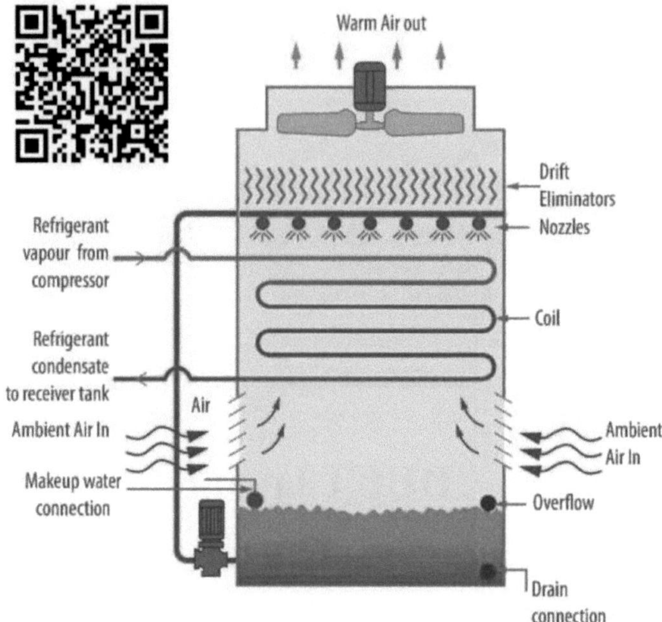

evaporative condenser

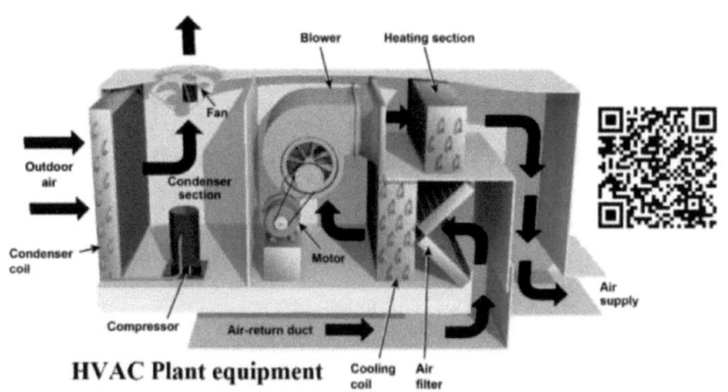

HVAC Plant equipment

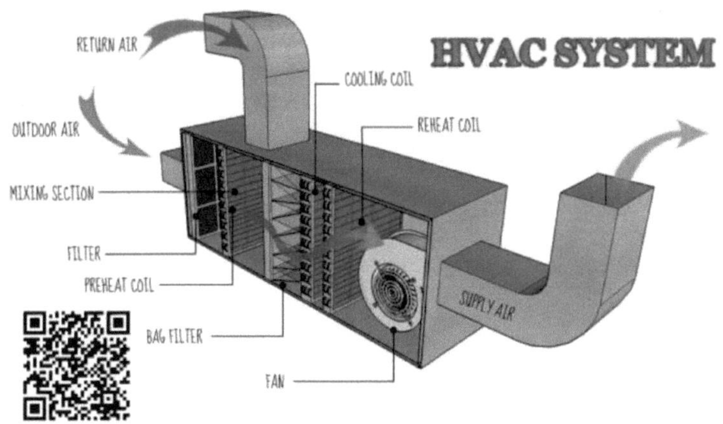

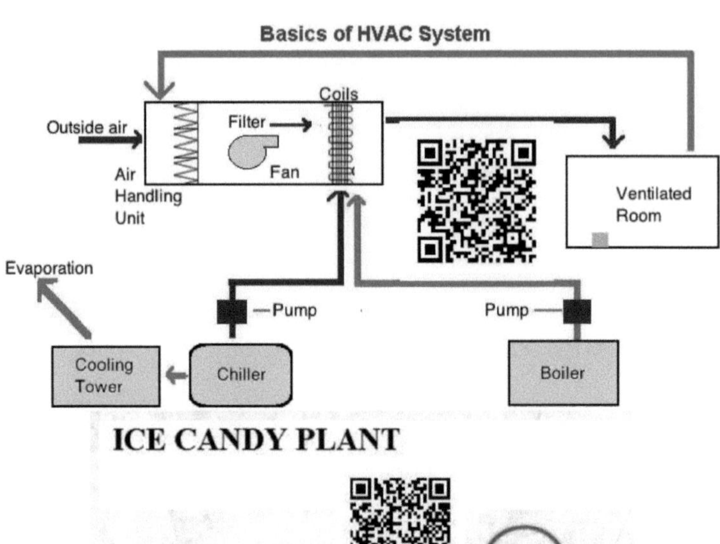
Basics of HVAC System
Coils
Outside air
Filter
Fan
Air
Handling
Unit
Ventilated
Room
Evaporation
Pump
Pump
Cooling
Tower
Chiller
Boiler

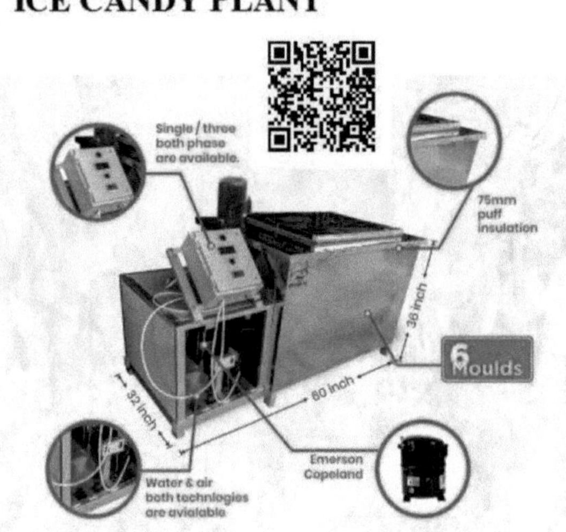
ICE CANDY PLANT
Single / three
both phase
are available.
75mm
puff
insulation
36 inch
6
Moulds
60 inch
32 inch
Emerson
Copeland
Water & air
both technlogies
are avialable

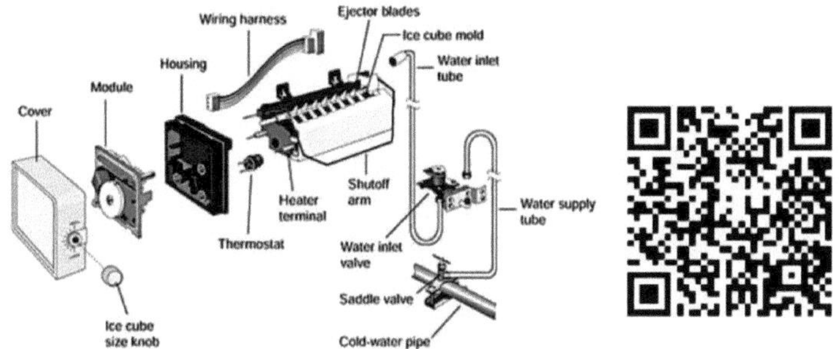

ICE CUBE MACHINE

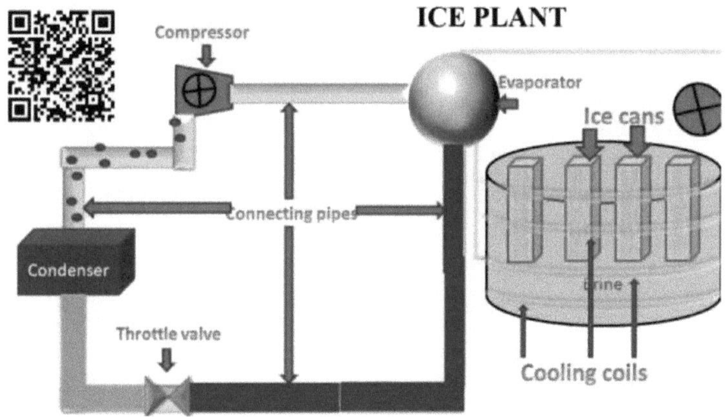

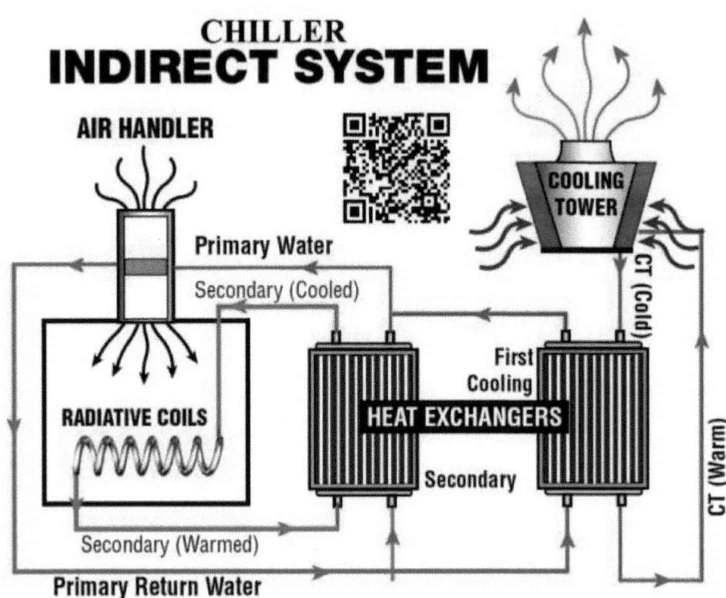
CHILLER
INDIRECT SYSTEM
AIR HANDLER
COOLING
TOWER
Primary Water
Secondary (Cooled)
CT (Cold)
First
Cooling
RADIATIVE COILS
HEAT EXCHANGERS
Secondary
CT (Warm)
Secondary (Warmed)
Primary Return Water

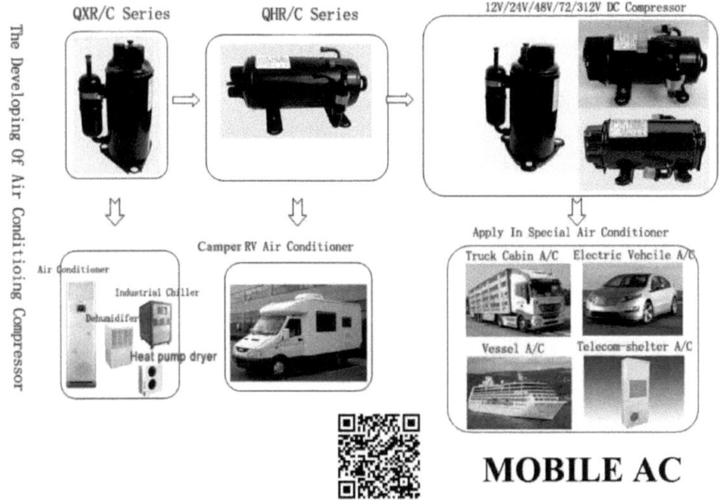
The Developing Of Air Conditioing Compressor
QXR/C Series
QHR/C Series
12V/24V/48V/72/312V DC Compressor
Air Conditioner
Industrial Chiller
Dehumidifer
Heat pump dryer
Camper RV Air Conditioner
Apply In Special Air Conditioner
Truck Cabin A/C
Electric Vehcile A/C
Vessel A/C
Telecom-shelter A/C
MOBILE AC

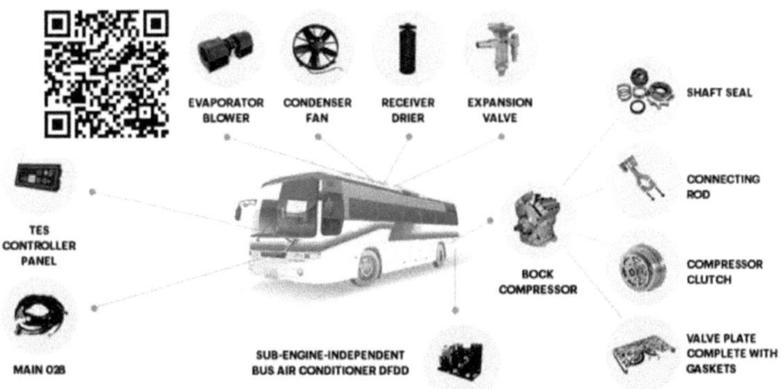
BUS A/C PARTS
For after-sales bus air conditioner market, offering various HVAC parts to repair your bus, coach, truck, van, RV, all-electric aircon system: bus A/C compressors, condenser fan, evaporator blower, clutch, Danfoss Parts etc.
EVAPORATOR BLOWER
CONDENSER FAN
RECEIVER DRIER
EXPANSION VALVE
SHAFT SEAL
CONNECTING ROD
COMPRESSOR CLUTCH
VALVE PLATE COMPLETE WITH GASKETS
BOCK COMPRESSOR
TES CONTROLLER PANEL
MAIN 02B
SUB-ENGINE-INDEPENDENT BUS AIR CONDITIONER DFDD

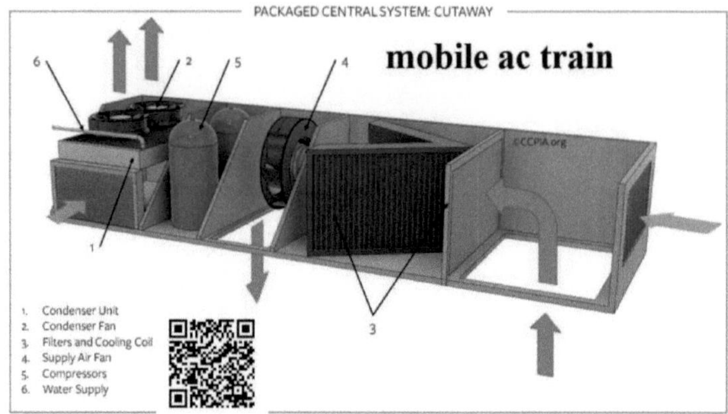
PACKAGED CENTRAL SYSTEM: CUTAWAY
mobile ac train
6
2
5
4
©CCPIA.org
1
3
1. Condenser Unit
2. Condenser Fan
3. Filters and Cooling Coil
4. Supply Air Fan
5. Compressors
6. Water Supply

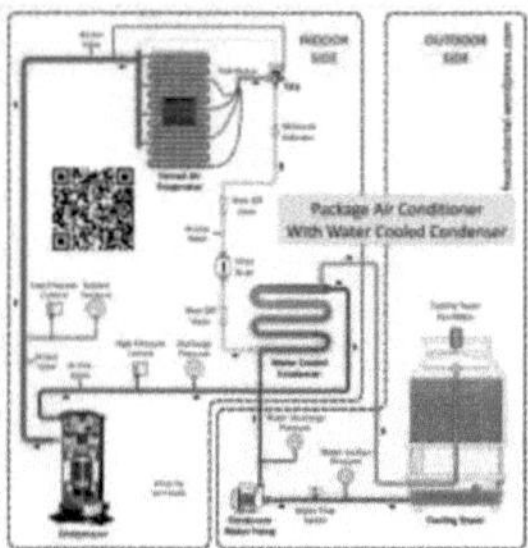
INDOOR SIDE
OUTDOOR SIDE
Package Air Conditioner
With Water Cooled Condenser

Cover of the hopper
Control Panle
Drip trap
Switch
Discharge door
Leakage holder
Truckle
The front truckle with brakes
softy machine

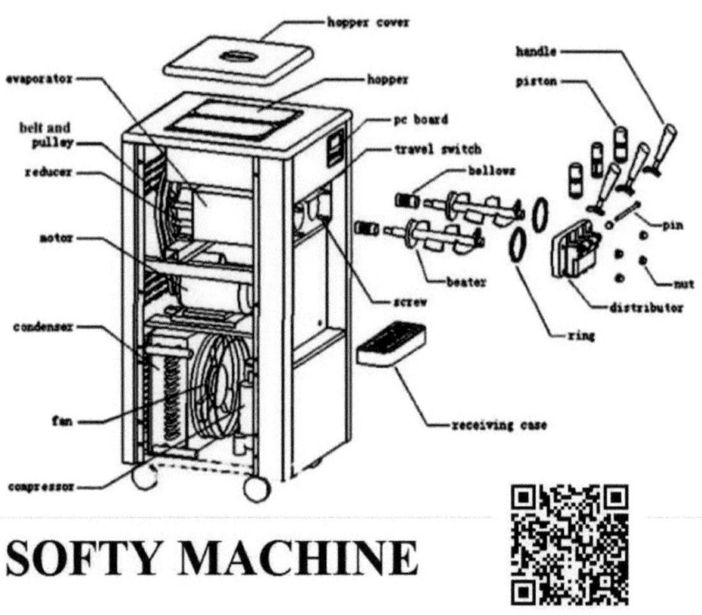

SOFTY MACHINE

SPLIT PACKAGE

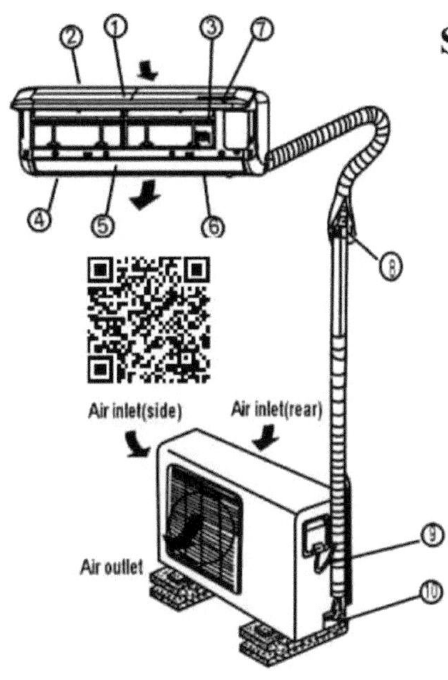

Names of parts

Indoor unit

1. Front panel
2. Air inlet
3. Air filter
4. Air outlet
5. Horizontal air flow grille
6. Vertical air flow louver(inside)
7. Display panel

Outdoor unit

8. Connecting pipe
9. Connecting cable
10. Stop valve

What is a split system?

Many types of air conditioning systems are called split systems because they are made up of an **outdoor unit,** which contains the condenser and compressor, and an **indoor unit,** which is often connected to a furnace or heat pump.

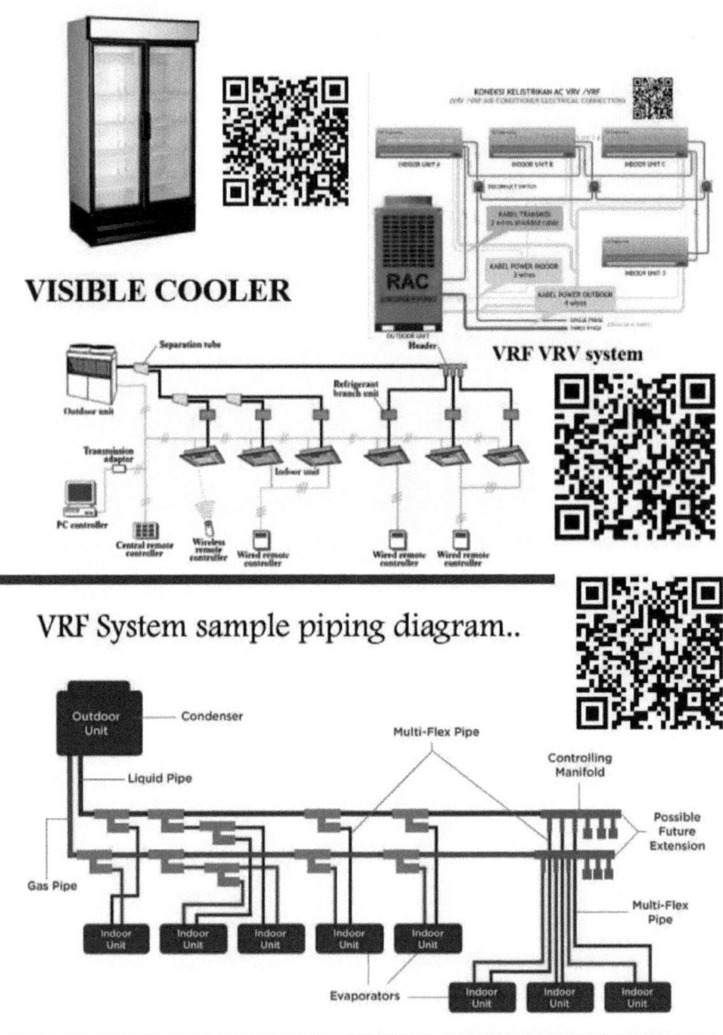
VISIBLE COOLER
RAC
Separation tube
Header
Outdoor unit
Refrigerant branch unit
Transmission adapter
Indoor unit
PC controller
Central remote controller
Wireless remote controller
Wired remote controller
Wired remote controller
Wired remote controller
VRF VRV system
VRF System sample piping diagram..
Outdoor Unit
Condenser
Multi-Flex Pipe
Liquid Pipe
Controlling Manifold
Possible Future Extension
Gas Pipe
Multi-Flex Pipe
Indoor Unit
Indoor Unit
Indoor Unit
Indoor Unit
Indoor Unit
Evaporators
Indoor Unit
Indoor Unit
Indoor Unit

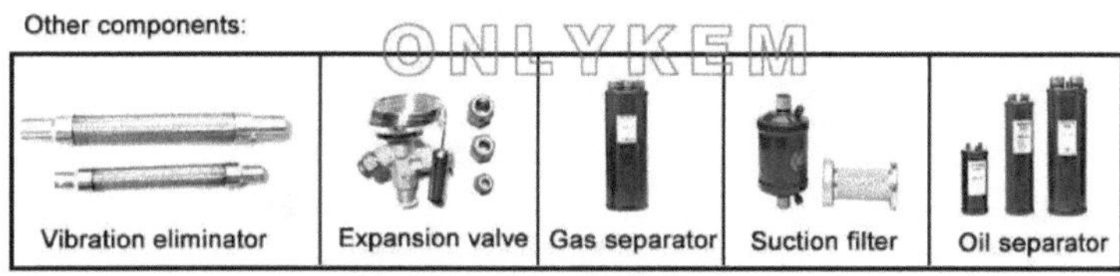

WALK IN COOLER

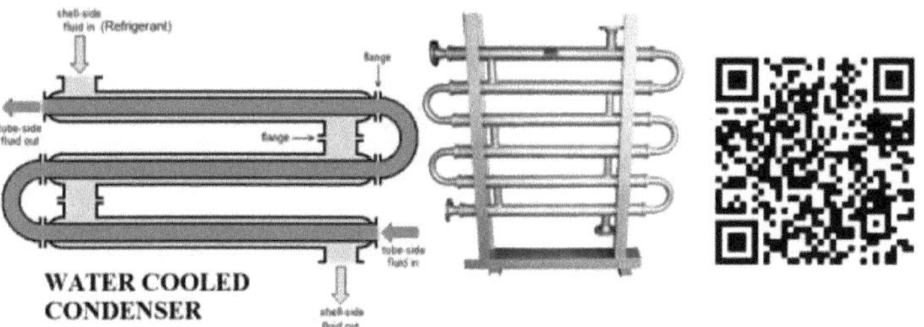

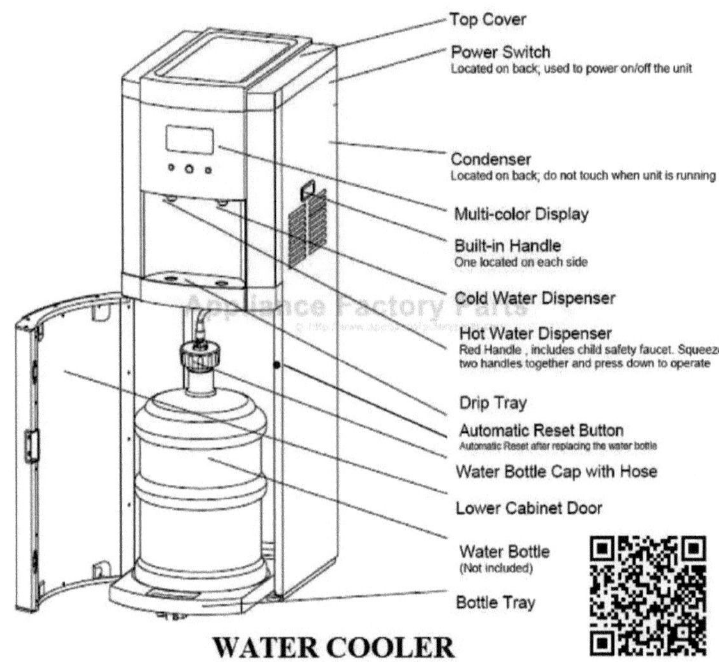

WATER COOLER

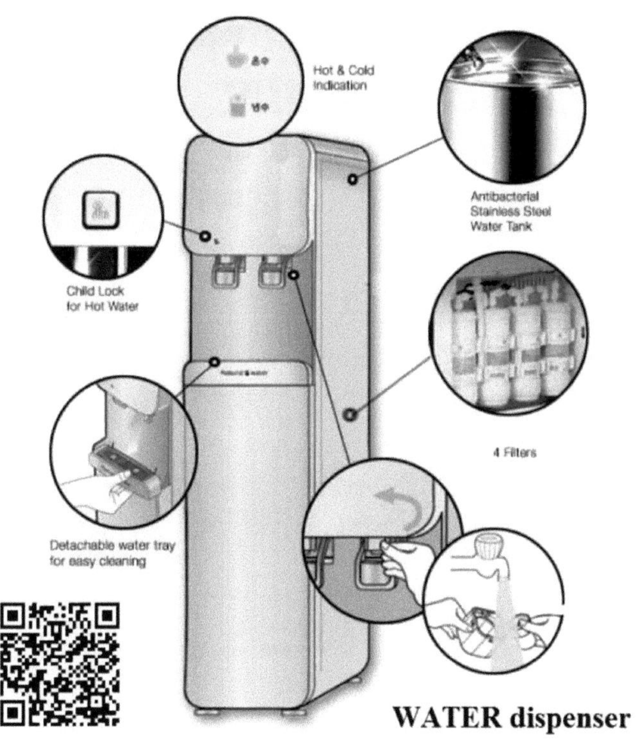
Hot & Cold
Indication
Antibacterial
Stainless Steel
Water Tank
Child Lock
for Hot Water
4 Filters
Detachable water tray
for easy cleaning
WATER dispenser

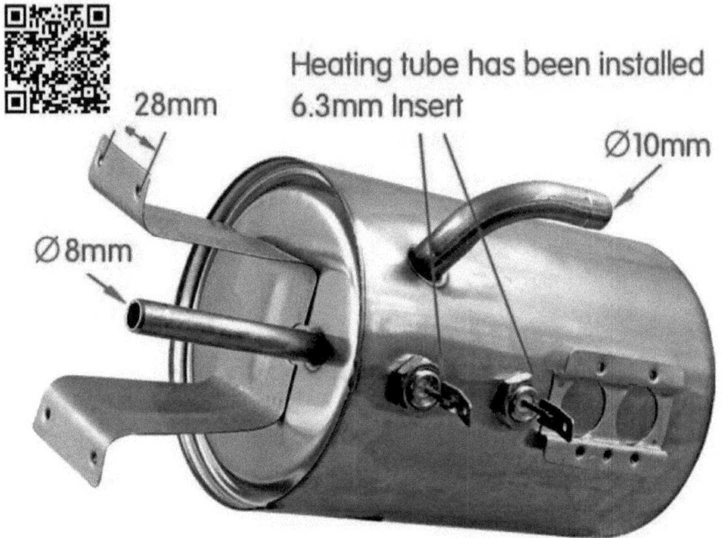
Water dispenser heating tank
Upper water outlet
Heating tube has been installed
28mm
6.3mm Insert
Ø10mm
Ø8mm

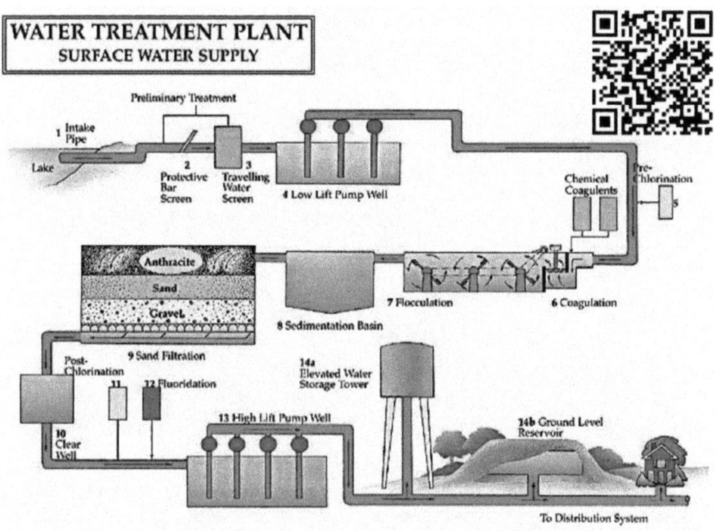
WATER TREATMENT PLANT
SURFACE WATER SUPPLY
Preliminary Treatment
1 Intake Pipe
Lake
2 Protective Bar Screen
3 Travelling Water Screen
4 Low Lift Pump Well
Chemical Coagulents
Pre-Chlorination
5
Anthracite
Sand
Gravel
8 Sedimentation Basin
7 Flocculation
6 Coagulation
9 Sand Filtration
Post-Chlorination
11
12 Fluoridation
10 Clear Well
14a Elevated Water Storage Tower
13 High Lift Pump Well
14b Ground Level Reservoir
To Distribution System

CHAPTER TWO

Refrigeration and Air Condition Technician Second Year MCQ

Q 1) Which component creates flow of refrigerant in the system

1) <u>Compressor</u>
2) Evaporator
3) Condenser
4) Expansion valve

Q 2) A hermetically sealed compressor does not start when switched on and its motor does not hum. This could be due to ....

1) Faulty starting capacitor
2) <u>Open - circuited motor windings</u>
3) Low supply voltage
4) A seized up compressor _

Q 3) Thermo - compressor works on ....

1) Pascal s Law
2) <u>Bernoulli s Principle</u>
3) Dalton s Law
4) Avogadro s Law

Q 5) Which control provided in a refrigerator protects the compressor motor winding from damage

1) Starting relay
2) <u>Overload protector</u>
3) Thermostat
4) All of the above

Q 6) In absorption refrigeration system, the compressor of vapour compression system is replaced by ....

1) Absorber

2) Generator

3) Pump

4) All the above

Q 7) One of the desirable properties of refrigerant is that it should have ......

1) Low critical temperature

2) Low specific heat

3) Low thermal conductivity

4) Low electrical insulation

Q 8) Which of these refrigerants has the lowest Relative Ozone Destruction Efficiency

1) R - 11

2) R - 12

3) R - 22

4) R - 114

Q 9) A plate type evaporator is often used in a ....

1) Domestic air conditioner

2) Drinking water cooler

3) Domestic dehumidifier

4) Two-compartment refrigerator

Q 10) In a domestic refrigerator, the expansion valve used is ....

1) Capillary tube

2) Constant pressure expansion valve

3) Thermostatic expansion valve

4) Float valve

Q 11) In a flooded type chiller application, the expansion valve used is ....

1) Capillary tube

2) Constant pressure expansion valve

3) Thermostatic expansion valve

4) Float valve

Q 12) Ammonia is also known as ....

1) R707

2) R717

3) R727

4) R737

Q 14) What is true about zener diode

1) It is a rectifier

2) It is light emitting diode

3) It is used in voltage regulator circuits

4) It is used in filter circuit

Q 15) A transformer is a device which can ....

1) Step up or step down voltage

2) Work through electric induction

3) Work without changing power

4) Do all the above

Q 16) 3 - Phase induction motor will have .... power factor during no load conditions

1) Low

2) Moderate

3) High

4) Negative

Q 17) Which induction motor has better starting torque

1) Slip ring induction motor has better starting torque than squirrel cage induction motor

2) Squirrel cage induction motor has better starting torque than slip ring induction motor

3) Both have similar starting torque

4) Any one of the two can have better starting torque than the other

Q 18) The undercharging of refrigerant in a refrigerator will cause ....

1) Increase in COP

2) Decrease in COP

3) Increase in capacity

4) It will have no effect

Q 19) Which compressor is suitable for large capacity and high volume flow rate

1) Screw compressor

2) Scroll compressor

3) Centrifugal compressor

4) Reciprocating compressor

Q 20) During expansion in capillary tube, the enthalpy ....

1) Increases

2) Decreases

3) Remains the same

4) May increase or decrease

Q 21) The HFC refrigerant is ....

1) R11

2) R22

3) R134a

4) R290

Q 22) The capacity of a domestic refrigerator is approximately ....

1) 0.1 ton

2) O.5 ton

3) 1.0 ton

4) 1.5 ton

Q 23) The material used for production of fibreglass insulation is ....

1) Carbon

2) Pumice

3) Gypsum

4) Silica

Q 24) The insulating material which is NOT used in domestic refrigerator is .....

1) Wood fibre

2) Cork

3) Rubber

4) Glass wool

Q 25) Leakage in the refrigeration system using ammonia as refrigerant is detected by

1) Soap and water

2) Sulphur sticks

3) Halide torch

4) Burning candle

Q 26) What is the cause of refrigerant contamination

1) Moisture in refrigerant

2) Low oil level

3) High oil level

4) Short of gas

Q 27) The function of air diffuser in air conditioning is to ....

1) Clean air

2) Direct air flow in desired pattern

3) Reduce noise of air conditioner

4) Control relative humidity of air

Q 28) In flooded type of evaporator, expansion device used is ....

1) Non return valve

2) Float valve

3) Thermostatic device

4) Self-actuated expansion valve

Q 29) Which statement is NOT true about Vortex Tube (non conventional) refrigerating system

1) It uses air as refrigerant

2) It is light in weight

3) It requires less space

4) It has a number of moving parts

Q 30) Which of these is an example of application of Vortex Tube refrigerating system

1) Spot cooling of electronic components

2) Body cooling of workers in mines

3) Both of the above

4) None of the above

Q 31) The working fluid mostly chosen in Pulse - tube refrigeration is ....

1) Helium

2) Carbon dioxide

3) Nitrogen

4) Ammonia

Q 32) In lithium-bromide vapour absorption refrigeration system, lithium bromide is used as

1) Refrigerant

2) Absorbent

3) Both as absorbent and refrigerant

4) Neither as absorbent nor as refrigerant

Q 33) Which of these methods cannot be used for starting 3-phase squirrel cage induction motor

1) DOL starter

2) Auto transformer starter

3) Star - delta starter

4) Rotor resistor starting

Q 35) In ice manufacturing, ice cans are fabricated from ....

1) Aluminium

2) Copper
3) Brass
4) Galvanized steel

Q 36) Which one of these compressors has poor partial load efficiency
1) Scroll compressor
2) Reciprocating compressor
3) Screw compressor
4) Centrifugal compressor

Q 37) The filters that are generally used to remove vapours, harmful chemicals, odour from compressed air system are
1) Hopkalite filters
2) Sterile filters
3) Coalescing filters
4) Adsorption activated carbon filters

Q 38) Oil - free (no lubrication) compressors are ....
1) Reciprocating compressor
2) Screw compressors
3) Centrifugal compressor
4) All of the above

Q 39) What method is used to control the capacity of water-cooled condenser
1) Vary temperature of water entering the condenser
2) Use variable-speed drive on the condenser water pump
3) Use diverting valve andpipe to bypass the condenser
4) All of the above

Q 40) The change in enthalpy that occurs in the .... is called the refrigeration effect.
1) Compressor
2) Condenser
3) Evaporator
4) Expansion device

Q 41) The heat rejection capacity of a condenser is affected by the following, except
1) Maximum pressure occuring at the condenser
2) Flow rate of cooling media in the condenser
3) Temperature difference between refrigerant and cooling media
4) Rate of flow of refrigerant in the condenser

Q 42) If the flow rate of refrigerant is high, which compressor will you choose

1) Reciprocating compressor
2) Centrifugal compressor
3) Screw compressor
4) Rotary compressor

Q 43) Performance of cooling tower is affected significantly by these factors, except .....

1) Approach
2) Wet bulb temperature
3) The range
4) TDS

Q 44) Inside cooling tower, a material is added to increase contact surface and contact time betwwen air and water. What is this material called

1) Insert
2) Pack
3) Fill
4) Core

Q 45) The disinfectants which can be used to get rid of viruses and bacteria are

1) Chlorine and water
2) Chlorine and ozone
3) Ultraviolet light and air
4) Ultraviolet light and water _

Q 46) For small evaporators where refrigerant used is other than ammonia, tubing used is made of..

1) Steel
2) Copper
3) Brass
4) Bronze

Q 47) Why is it NOT recommended to clean condenser fins with a hose

1) Water will turn dirt into mud which will be hard to clean
2) Water will make the fins rust very quickly
3) Using hose is not bad. Recommendation need not be accepted
4) Using hose hardly does any damage to fins

Q 48) Why is it desirable for refrigerant entering the compressor to be slightly superheated

1) To prevent refrigerant oil from leaving the compressor

2) To prevent vapour refrigerant from entering the compressor

3) To keep compressor warm

4) To prevent liquid refrigerant from entering the compressor

Q 50) The purpose of HVAC system is to control ....

1) Temperature and humidity only

2) Supply of outside air

3) Air filtration and its movement in occupied spaces

4) All of the above

Q 52) As per heat load calculation, the load of AC II tier railway coach is about ....

1) 4 ton

2) 14 ton

3) 12 ton

4) 16 ton

Q 53) Which refrigerant is used in automotive air conditioning

1) Ammonia

2) carbon dioxide

3) Freon

4) Brine

Q 54) On a vehicle with V belts, an intermittent sequealing noise is heard on acceleration with the AC control switch on or off position. The most likely cause for this problem is

1) A loose power steering belt

2) A loose AC compressor belt

3) A loose air pump belt

4) A worn AC compressor pulley bearing

Q 55) Secondary refrigerant is invariably used in ....

1) Domestic refrigerator

2) Ice plant

3) Deep freezer

4) Water cooler

Q 56) The most common insulating material in cold storage is ....

1) PUF

2) Thermocole

3) Cork

4) Glass wool

Q 57) The type of duct which requires least material for carrying air is ....

1) Square
2) Rectaangular
3) Circular
4) Trapezoidal

Q 58) ______________signs are triangular in shape.
1) Warning
2) Informative
3) Mandatory
4) Prohibitive

Q 59) 1 tonne of refrigeration is equal to____________of power.
1) 3.52 kW
2) 1.05 kW
3) 211 kW
4) 232 kW

Q 60) Which of these in a Vapour absorption refrigeration system, converts ammonia vapour into liquid ammonia
1) Condenser
2) Evaporator
3) Absorber
4) Analyser

Q 61) _______________regulates the temperature inside the refrigeration cabinet.
1) Thermostat switch
2) Split phase motor
3) Relay
4) Overload protector

Q 63) Which of these capacity control methods of a compressor is also known as Cylinder unloader
1) Use of multiple units
2) Speed modulation
3) Hot gas bypass
4) ON OFF control

Q 65) The amount of water vapour present in a kilogram of dry air in the atmosphere is called __
1) specific humidity
2) air saturation
3) moist point
4) dry mass

Q 66) When the air is in saturated state, the value of wet bulb depression is________

1) zero

2) negative

3) maximum

4) unity

Q 67) To maintain human comfort, the value of air stratification should be kept __________

1) minimum

2) maximum

3) infinity

4) negative

Q 68) Which of the following facts is FALSE about Rigid Duct

1) Flexible

2) Expensive

3) Heavy

4) Water proof

Q 70) Sensible heat load is the product of sensible load, ___________and _____________

1) heat transmission factor, temperature

2) latent heat, temperature

3) temperature difference, mass

4) heat transmission factor, mass

1]Pick up the wrong statement] A refrigerant should have

(a)Tow specific heat of liquid

(b)high boiling point

(c)high latent heat of vaporisation

(d)higher critical temperature

Q 2) At constant pressure, volume varies as the temperature of the gas. This is statement of .....

1) Boyle s Law

2) Charles Law

3) Joule-Thompson Effect

4) Dalton s Law

Q 3) One ton of refrigeration = ...

1) 45.5 kcal min.

2) 50.4 kcal min.

3) 44.5 kcal min.

4) 66.5 kcal min

Q 4) The amount of heat required to raise the temperature of a unit mass of a substance through 1 degree C is called ....

1) Specific heat
2) Sensible heat
3) Latent heat
4) Superheat

Q 5) If the relative humidity of air is 100%, the rate of evaporation will be .....

1) High
2) Medium
3) Low
4) Zero

Q 6) Capillary tube is a device which ....

1) Removes heat carried by the refrigerant
2) Meters the refrigerant
3) Acts as a reservoir for excess liquid refrigerant
4) Pumps the refrigeerant

Q 7) The heart of the refrigeration system is ....

1) Liquid receiver
2) Thermostat
3) Compressor
4) Evaporator

Q 8) Drier used to remove the moisture contents from the liquid refrigerant is charged with ......

1) Silica gel
2) Calcium carbide
3) Clay absorber
4) Ethylene absorber

Q 9) Which of these is not a brine

1) Sodium chloride
2) Calcium chloride
3) Ethylene glycol
4) None of the above

Q 10) A micrometer has a positive error of 0.02 mm. If it reads 25.41 mm, correct reading is .....

1) 25.39 mm
2) 25.37 mm

3) 25.43 mm

4) 25.45 mm

Q 12) Thickness of sheet metal is indicated by a series of numbers called ....

1) Standard size

2) Number size

3) <u>Gauge</u>

4) Normal size

Q 13) One of the functions of welding electrode coating is to ....

1) Increase welding current

2) <u>Stabilize the arc</u>

3) Prevent rusting

4) Control arc temperature

Q 15) The butter compartment of a domestic refrigerator is normally located ......

1) At the top of the cabinet

2) At the bottom of the cabinet

3) At the central height

4) <u>In the door</u>

Q 16) Evaporation process takes place in the evaporator, because of which .....

1) Heat gets added

2) <u>Heat is removed</u>

3) Pressure increases

4) Pressure decreases

Q 17) Snip is a ....

1) Measuring tool

2) Marking tool

3) <u>Cutting tool</u>

4) Supporting tool

Q 18) The unit of frequency is ....

1) Mho

2) Coulomb

3) <u>Hertz</u>

4) Tesla

Q 19) The compressor used in refrigerator is ....

1) <u>Hermetically sealed reciprocating compressor</u>

2) Semi-hermetically sealed reciprocating compressor

3) Open type compressor
4) Centrifugal compressor

Q 20) Domestic refrigerator works on ....
1) Vapour compression cycle
2) Vapour absorption cycle
3) Otto cycle
4) Vapour compression or vapour absorption cycle

Q 21) Which is more efficient - water cooled or air cooled condenser
1) Air cooled
2) Water cooled
3) Both are equally efficient
4) Any one can be more efficient than the other

Q 22) This is NOT a desirable property of insulating material.
1) Resistance to water
2) High thermal conductivity
3) Non-flammable
4) Light in weight

Q 23) One of the complaints against use of window air conditioner is that it is ....
1) Expensive
2) Difficult to install
3) Difficult to maintain
4) Noisy

Q 24) Which of these is NOT a part of outside unit of a split air conditioner
1) Evaporator coil
2) Condenser coil
3) Compressor
4) Expansion coil

Q 25) In a refrigeration cycle, heat is rejected by refrigerant at ....
1) Condenser
2) Evaporator
3) Compressor
4) Expansion valve

Q 26) Which of these is a semi-conductor
1) Gold
2) Lead

3) Silicon
4) Plastic
Q 27) The cooling effect in a cooling tower can be increased by ....
1) Increasing velocity of air over wet surface
2) Lowering barometric pressure
3) Reducing humidity of air
4) All of the above
Q 28) CRO gives ....
1) Actual representation
2) Visual representation
3) Approximate representation
4) Incorrect representation
Q 29) Integrated circuits are normally made of ....
1) Silicon
2) Germanium
3) Copper
4) Aluminium
Q 30) The active components in an IC are ....
1) Resistors
2) Capacitors
3) Transistors and diodes
4) None of the above
2]A standard ice point temperature corresponds to the temperature of
(a)water at 0°C
(b)ice at 4°C
(c)solid and dry ice
(e)mixture of ice and water Under equilibrium conditions]
3]Vapour compression refrigeration is some what like
(a)Carnot cycle
(b)Rankine cycle
(c)reversed Camot cycle
(e)none of the above]
4]Which of the following cycles uses air as the refrigerant
(a)Ericsson
(b)Stirling
(c)Carnot
(d)Bellcoleman
5]Ammoniaabsorption refrigeration cycle requires

(a)very little work input
(b)maximum work input
(c)nearly same work input as for vapour compression cycle
(d)zero work input
6]An important characteristic of absorption system of refrigeration is
(a)noisy operation
(b)quiet operation
(c)cooling below 0°C
(d)very little power consumption
8]Clapeyron equation is a relation between
(a)temperature, pressure and enthalpy
(b)specific volume and enthalpy
(c)temperature and enthalpy
(e)temperature, pressure, specific volur and'enthalpy]
19]Clapeyron equation is applicable for registration at
(a)saturation point of vapour
(b)saturation point of liquid
(c)sublimation temperature
(d)triple point
(e)critical point]
10] In vapour compression cycle, the conditii of refrigerant is saturated liquid
(a)after passing through the condenser
(b)before passing through the condensei
(c)after passing through the expansion throttle valve
(d)before entering the expansion valve
11] In vapour compression cycle, the condition of refrigerant is very wet vapour
(a)after passing through the condenser
(b)before passing through the condenser
(c)after passing through the expansion or throttle valve
(e)before entering the compressor]
12] In vapour compression cycle, the condition of refrigerant is high pressure saturated liquid
(a)after passing through the condenser
(b)before passing through the condenser
(c)after passing through the expansion or thiottle valve
(d)before entering the expansion valve

13] In vapour compression cycle the condition of refrigerant is superheated vapour

(a)after passing through the condenser

(b)before passing through the condenser

(c)after passing through the expansion or throttle valve

(d)before [entering the expansion valve

14] In vapour compression cycle the condition off refrigerant is dry saturated vapour

(a)after passing through the condenser

(b)before passing through the condenser

(c)after passing through the expansion or throttle valve

(e)before entering the compressor]

15] The boiling point of ammonia is

(a)100°C

(b)50°C

(c) 33]3°C

(d)0°C

(e)33]3°C]

16] One ton of refrigeration is equal to the refrigeration effect corresponding to melting of 1000 kg of ice

(a)in 1 hour

(b) in 1 minute

(c)in 24 hours

(d)in 12 hours

17] One ton refrigeratiqn corresponds to

(a)50 kcal/min

(b) 50 kcal/kr

(c) 80 kcal/min

(d) 80 kcal/hr

18] In S]J] unit, one ton of refrigeration is equal to

(a) 210 kJ/min

(b) 21 kJ/min

(c) 420 kJ/min

(d) 840 kJ/min

19]The vapour compression refrigerator employs the following cycie

(a) Rankine

(b) Carnot

(c)Reversed Rankine

(e)Reversed Carnot]

20]Allowable pressure on highpressure side or ammonia absorption system is of the order of

(a)atmospheric pressure

(b)slightly above atmospheric pressure

(c)24 bars

(d)56 bars

21]The moisture in a refrigerant is removed by

(a) evaporator

(b)safety relief valve

(c) dehumidifier

(d)driers

Q 31) Temporary hardness of water is removed by ....

1) Filtering

2) Boiling

3) Chemical treatment

4) None of the above

Q 32) Natural draft cooling towers are mainly used in ....

1) Steel plants

2) Power stations

3) Fertilizer plants

4) Aluminium manufacturing plants

Q 33) What is used in pre-treatment of water to remove large objects

1) Bacteria

2) Oil and grease

3) Air

4) Screen

Q 34) In the evaporator the refrigerant enters at ....

1) Very low pressure

2) Low pressure

3) Medium pressure

4) High pressure

Q 35) The type of evaporator used in large refrigeration and central air conditioning systems is

1) Shell and tube evaporator

2) Finned evaporator

3) Plate surface evaporator

4) Bare tube evaporator

Q 36) Why are ice cans made tapered in height

1) To reduce weight

2) To facilitate dumping

3) To improve appearance

4) To make fabrication easier

Q 37) The instrument used to measure relative humidity is ....

1) Barometer

2) Psychrometer

3) Manometer

4) Pressure gauge

Q 38) Pressure on the high pressure side of a mechanical refrigeration unit is called

1) Suction pressure

2) Discharge or head pressure

3) Differential pressure _

4) Absolute pressure _

Q 42) Dry bulb temperature (DBT) is the actual temperature of ....

1) Moist air

2) Dry air

3) Dry ice

4) Saturated air

Q 43) AHU stands for ....

1) Air Handling Unit

2) Air Heating Unit

3) Air Humidifying Unit

4) None of these

Q 44) Refrigeration is used in medical industry for_____________

1) storing blood

2) refining petroleum

3) production of ice

4) production of rocket fuel

Q 46) Which of the following tools is used to open and close the service valve

1) Cylindrical valve key

2) Pinching Tool

3) Punch set

4) Swagging Tool

Q 47) ______________is a cutting tool used to make the metal surface smooth.

1) File
2) Hacksaw
3) Scriber
4) Trammel

Q 48) Which of these is used to make deep holes in the wood

1) Gimlet
2) Stake
3) Snap
4) Mallet

Q 49) Which of the following device measures electric current in a circuit

1) Ammeter
2) Wattmeter
3) Voltmeter
4) Watt-hour meter

Q 50) ______________is not an insulator.

1) Eureka
2) Asbestos
3) Ebonite
4) Glass

Q 51) The unit of Impedance is________________.

1) Ohm
2) Ohm-metre
3) Henry
4) Farad

Q 52) Universal A.C. motor provides__________torque and operates at ___________speed.

1) high, high
2) high, low
3) low, high
4) low, low

Q 53) At which of the following places, slip ring motors are used 1. planer 2. crane 3. lathe 4. grinder slotter Select the correct answer from the codes given below.

1) 1,2
2) 2,3

3) 1,2,3

4) 2,4

Q 54) _____________is primarily used in compressor.

1) Capacitor start capacitor run motor

2) Hysteresis motor

3) Shaded pole induction motor

4) Repulsion motor _

Q 55) P-type semiconductor cannot be made by adding ___________ with Germanium.

1) Arsenic

2) Indium

3) Gallium

4) Boron

Q 56) Laser diode finds its application in_____________

1) fibre amplifier

2) television receiver

3) remote controls

4) photo conductors

Q 58) Which of these is used as a charger in the machine used for refrigeration

1) Refrigerant adapter

2) Charging meter

3) Vaccum pump

4) Compressor oil charging pump

Q 59) In Vapour Absorption refrigeration, ______________is used for refrigeration.

1) Heat energy

2) Mechanical energy

3) Potential energy

4) Chemical energy

Q 61) Compressors cannot be classified a____________according to the method of compression.

1) Multi stage compressor

2) Reciprocating compressor

3) Rotating compressor

4) Centrifugal compressor

22]The condensing pressure due to the presence of noncondensable gases, as compared to that actually required forcondensing temperatures without noncondensable gases,

(a) will be higher

(b) will be lower

(c)will remain unaffected

(d)may be higher or lower depending upon the nature of non-condensable gases

23]Critical pressure of a liquid is the pressure

(a)above which liquid will remain liquid

(b)above which liquid becomes gas

(c)above which liquid becomes vapour

(d)above which liquid becomes solid

24]Critical temperature is' the temperature above which

(a) a gas will never liquefy

(b) a gas will immediately liquefy

(c)water will evaporate

(d)water will never evaporate

25]The refrigerant for a refrigerator should have

(a) high sensible heat

(b) high total heatFluid

(c) high latent heat

(d)low latent heat

26]Rating of a domestic refrigerator is of the order of

(a)0]1 ton

(b) 5 tons

(c)10 tons

(d)40 tons

27]The COP of a domestic refrigerator

(a)is less than 1

(b)is more than 1

(c)is equal to 1

(d)depends upon the make

28]The domestic refrigerator uses following type of compressor

(a) centrifugal

(b)axial

(c)miniature sealed unit

(d)piston type reciprocating

29]Presence of moisture in a refrigerant affects the working of

(a) compressor

(b) condenser

(c) evaparator

(d) expansion valve]

30]Refrigeration in aeroplanes usually employs the following refrigerant

(a) Co2

(b)Freon11

(c) Freon22

(d)Air

31]Domestic refrigerator working on vapour compression cycle uses the following type of expansion device

(a)electrically operated throttling valve

(b)manually operated valve

(c)thermostatic valve

(d)capillary tube

32]Air refrigeration operates on

(a)Carnot cycle

(b)Reversed Carnot cycle

(c)Rankine cycle

(e)Brayton cycle]

33]Air refrigeration cycle is used in

(a)domestic refrigerators

(b)commercial refrigerators

(c)air conditioning

(d)gas liquefaction

34]In a vapour compression cycle, the refrigerant immediately after expansion valve is

(a) liquid

(b) subcooled liquid

(c)saturated liquid

(d)wet vapour

35]The vapour pressure of refrigerant should be

(a)lower than atmospheric pressure

(b)higher than atmospheric pressure

(c)equal to atmospheric

(d)could be anything

36]For better COP of refrigerator, the pressure range corresponding to temperature in evaporator and condenser must be

(a)small

(b)high

(c)euqal

(d)anything

37]The bank of tubes at the back of domestic refrigerator are

(a)condenser tubes

(b)evaporator tubes

(c)refrigerant cooling tubes

(d)capillary tubes

38]The higher temperature in vapour compression cycle occurs at

(a)receiver

(b) expansion valve

(c) evaporator

(e)compressor discharge]

39]Highest temperature encountered in refrigeration cycle should be

(a)near critical temperature of refrigerant

(b)above critical temperature

(c)at critica] temperature

(d)much below critical temperature

40]In refrigerator, liquid receiver is required between condenser and flow controlling device, if quantity of refrigerant forsystem is

(a)less than 2 kg

(b)more than or equal to 3]65 kg

(c)more than 10 kg

(d)there is no such consideration

Q 62) The efficiency of centrifugal compressors as compared to that of reciprocating compressors is

1) high

2) low

3) equal

4) low or equal

Q 63) Which of the following compressors are primarily considered as the most appropriate for refrigerant fluid

1) Scroll compressor

2) Hermetically sealed compressor

3) Swash plate compressor

4) Wobble plate compressor

Q 64) Wet compression____________the compressor efficiency.

1) increases

2) decreases

3) halves

4) has no effect on

Q 65) Water cooled condensers have ____________heat transfer rate as compared to air cooled condensers.

1) high

2) low

3) equal

4) low or equal

Q 66) Which of these is a tank shaped device used for storing liquid refrigerant in refrigeration

1) Liquid receiver

2) Condenser

3) Compressor oil charging pump

4) Evaporator

Q 67) The compressor compresses the refrigerant to high pressure to______________

1) increase the temperature

2) heat the refrigerant

3) decrease the temperature

4) condense the refrigerant

Q 68) Both air and water are used as cooling medium in __________________ condenser.

1) evaporative

2) shell and tube

3) shell and coil

4) air cooled

Q 69) Plate surface evaporators are not used in____________

1) food processing industry

2) ice-cream cabinet -

3) domestic refrigerator

4) freezer

Q 70) In order to prevent the quantity of liquid refrigerant present in the refrigerant obtained from evaporator from entering into the condenser, ____________is connected between evaporator and compressor.

1) accumulator

2) superheater

3) bottle cooler

4) water cooler

Q 71) In reverse cycle defrosting, evaporator works like a_____________.

1) Condenser

2) evaporator itself

3) expansion valve

4) accumulator

Q 72) Where do the automatic expansion valves find their application

1) In domestic refrigerator

2) In food processing units

3) In air conditioners

4) In ice-cream plants

Q 73) Change of pressure of capillary tube is __________ the diameter of capillary tube.

1) directly proportional to

2) inversely proportional to

3) directly proportional to the square of

4) inversely proportional to the square of

Q 74) Which of the following removes moisture from refrigerant in an air-conditioning system

1) Drier

2) expansion valve

3) Condenser

4) capillary tube

Q 75) Which of these is a secondary refrigerant

1) Brine

2) Ammonia

3) Freon

4) Methyl chloride

Q 76) Chemical formula of Freon-12 is_____________.

1) CCl_2F_2

2) CF_2

3) CCl_2

4) CCl_4

Q 77) The refrigerant symbol for Methane (CH_4) is_____________

1) R-50

2) R-14

3) R-11

4) R-240

Q 78) ___________is not an anti-freeze substance. ____________

1) Methylene Chloride

2) Methyl Alcohol

3) Ethylene Glycol

4) Glycerine

Q 79) Which of these thermal insulations used in refrigeration has highest density

1) Calcium silicate

2) Cotton

3) Granulate

4) Wool

Q 80) ____________ is an outlet grill designed to guide the direction of air in the duct system.

1) diffuser

2) ejector

3) register

4) converter

Q 81) The free wheel used in automotive vehicles is also known as _____________

1) over running clutch

2) under running cluth

3) magnetic clutch

4) automatic clutch

Q 82) In a car A.C., compressor is connected with the __________.

1) engine

2) clutch

3) chasis

4) wheels

Q 83) If the split A.C. is giving insufficient air cooling, then which of the given is a possible reason

1) air filter is dirty

2) timer setting is changed

3) main supply is defective

4) outer temperature is low

Q 84) __________measures pressure and vaccum in an air conditioning system.

1) Compound gauge

2) Vaccum gauge

3) Tachometer

4) Pressure gauge

Q 85) In a window air conditioner, __________evaporator is used.

1) fin type

2) coil type

3) spiral

4) duct-type

Q 86) In case of damage in compressor of a refrigeration system and blockage of dryer etc., ___________ is done.

1) retrofitting

2) suction

3) insulation

4) expansion

Q 87) Which of these amounts to the difference between moist temperature and real liquid refrigerant temperature

1) Sub-cooling

2) Superheating

3) Evaporation

4) Condensation

Q 88) Expansion valve controls the _______________________in the evaporator.

1) amount of refrigerant

2) temperature of system

3) temperature of refrigerant

4) pressure of system

Q 89) The part of a screw compressor to which the rotor is attached is called____________.

1) housing

2) driver

3) discharge port

4) casing

Q 90) What happens to the volumetric efficiency during a pressure drop in the compressor

1) It increases

2) It decreases

3) It remains unchanged

4) It may increase or decrease

41]Absorption system normally uses the following refrigerant

(a) Freon11

(b) Freon22

(c) C02

(e) ammonia]

42] One of the purposes of subcooling the liquid refrigerant is to

(a)reduce compressor overheating

(b)reduce compressor discharge temperature

(c)increase cooling effect

(d)ensure that only liquid and not the vapour enters the expansion (throttling) valve

43] The value of COP in vapour compression cycle is usually

(a)always less than unity

(b)always more than unity

(c)equal to unity

(d)any one of the above

44] In a refrigeration system, heat absorbed in comparison to heat rejected is

(a) more

(b) less

(c)same

(d)more for small capacity and less for high capacity

45] Condensing temperature in a refrigerator is the temperature

(a)of cooling medium

(b)of freezing zone

(c)of evaporator

(d)at which refrigerant gas becomes liquid

46] Formation of frost on evaporator in refrigerator

(a)results in loss of heat due to poor heat transfer

(b)increases heat transfer rate

(c)is immaterial

(d)can be avoided by proper design

47] In refrigerators, the temperature difference between the evaporating refrigerant and the medium being cooled shouldbe

(a)high, of the order of 25°

(b)as low as possible (3 to 11°C)

(c)zero

(d)any value

48]In a flooded evaporator refrigerator, an accumulator at suction of compressor is used to

(a)collect liquid refrigerant and prevent it from going to compressor

(b)detect liquid in vapour

(c)superheat the vapour

(d)collect vapours

49]Accumulators should have adequate volume to store refrigerant charge at least

(a)10%

(b) 25%

(c) 50%

(d) 75%

50]At lower temperatures and pressures, the latent heat of vaporisation of a refrigerant

(a) decreases

(b)increases

(c)remains same

(d)depends on other factors

51]A refrigeration cycle operates between condenser temperature of + 27°C and evaporator temperature of 23°C] TheCannot coefficient of performance of cycle will be

(a)0]2

(b)1]2

(c) 5

(d) 6

52]Which of the following is not a desirable property of a refrigerant

(a)high triiscibility with oil

(b)low boiling point

(c)good electrical conductor

(d)large latent heat

53]In vapour compression refrigeration system, refrigerant occurs as liquid between

(a)condenser and expansion valve

(b)compressor and evaporator

(c)expansion valve and evaporator

(d)compressor and condenser

54]Pick up the correct statement about giving up of heat from one medium to other in ammonia absorption system (a)strong solution to weak solution

(b)weak solution to strong solution

(c)strong solution to ammonia vapour

(d)ammonia vapour to weak solution

55]Efficiency of a Cornot engine is given as 80%] If the cycle direction be reversed, what will be the value of COP ofreversed Carnot cycle

(a)1]25

(b)0]8

(c)0]5

(d) 0]25

56]Highest pressure encountered in a refrigeration system should be

(a)critical pressure of refrigerant

(b)much below critical pressure

(c)much above critical pressure

(d)near critical pressure

57] If a heat pump cycle operates between the condenser temperature of +27°C and evaporator temperature of 23°C,then the Carnot COP will be

(a)0]2

(b)1]2

(c) 5

(d)6

58]A certain refrigerating system has a normal operating suction pressure of 10 kg/cm gauge and condensing pressure ofabout 67 kg/cm] The refrigerant used is

(a)Ammonia

(b) Carbon dioxide

(c)Freon

(d) Brine

59]Aqua ammonia is used as refrigerant in the following type of refrigeration system

(a)compression

(b)direct

(c) indirect

(d) absorption

60]If the evaporator temperature of a plant is lowered, keeping the condenser temperature constant, the h]p] ofcompressor required will be

(a)same

(b) more

(c)less

(d)more/less depending on rating

Q 91) What are the applications of commercial compressor 1. water coolers 2. cold storage 3. ice cube machine Out of the above options, which of these is are correct

1) 1,2,3

2) 2,3

3) 1,3

4) 1,2

Q 92) Stuck-up fault in a compressor means_______________.

1) compressor is working tightly

2) compressor is making noise

3) there is friction in compressor

4) compressor is not starting

Q 93) Which of the following is used to make the natural air enter the closed cooling tower

1) Fan

2) Blower _

3) Cooler

4) Air conditioner

Q 94) ______________are attached in a Natural draft cooling tower to control the flow of air.

1) Louvres

2) Spray nozzles

3) Header

4) Valve

Q 95) Operating cost of mechanical draft cooling towers are compared to natural draft is___

1) high

2) low

3) equal

4) incomparable

Q 96) Wet bulb temperature is ________________the cooling tower capacity.

1) inversely proportional

2) directly proportional

3) inversely propotional to the square of

4) directly proportional to the square of

Q 97) Sludge is usually formed due to______________.

1) Calcium Chloride

2) Zinc Chloride

3) Hydrochloric acid

4) Sulphuric acid

Q 98) Which of these is not an external treatment given to scale formation

1) Colloidal treatment

2) Ion exchange process

3) Zeolite process

4) Soda lime process

Q 99) In electric treatment of water, sealed glass bulbs filled with_____________vapours are placed in the system in order to block the scale formation process.

2) sodium

3) helium

4) argon

Q 101) The amount of refrigerant passed by the valve is____________the amount of refrigerant vapourized by the evaporator.

1) equal to

2) half

3) one-fourth

4) double

Q 102) _____________ is used as an expansion valve in a flooded evaporator.

1) Float valve

2) Thermostatic valve

3) Capillary tube

4) Orifice control valve

Q 103) Brine chiller is similar to___________of a vapour compression refrigeration system.

1) evaporator

2) Condenser

3) compressor

4) Capillary tube

Q 104) Condenser capacity is measured in_________

1) kW

2) kV

3) kVA
4) kA

Q 105) The capacity of condenser is not a function of________________
1) volume of refrigerant
2) surface area of condenser
3) overall heat transfer coefficient
4) temperature difference between refrigerant and condenser medium

Q 106) Cooling medium in Evaporative condenser is____________
1) both air and water
2) brine
3) air only
4) water only

Q 107) Wet bulb temperature is a measure of______________.
1) absolute humidity
2) absolute pressure
3) relative humidity
4) specific heat

Q 108) The temperature at which moisture in the air starts condensing is called____________.
1) dew point temperature
2) wet bulb temperature
3) dry bulb temperature
4) dew point depression

Q 109) _____________duct system is commonly used to obtain an efficient duct using friction method.
1) Rectangular
2) Square
3) Circular
4) Triangular

Q 110) Ducting done in large offices using____________type distribution.
1) Ceiling panel
2) Upward
3) Pan
4) Wall

Q 111) Which of these is NOT a probable reason for improper working of condenser unit
1) Temperature is not set

2) Condenser has become dirty

3) Air does not flow

4) Spray nozzle is closed

Q 112) The part of a duct used for joining two duct lines at right angle is called____________

1) stack elbow

2) outlet port

3) duct joint

4) tee joint

Q 113) In a direct expansion system, which of these is found in Plant room

2) Air filter

3) evaporator

4) Return air duct

Q 114) ____________is a device by which cool, clean and humid air can be obtained.

1) Air washer

2) Fan coil

3) Relief valve

4) Spray Nozzle

Q 115) ____________is installed in the circuit for usage of electromechanical controls.

1) Relay

2) Meggar

3) Circuit Breaker

4) Fuse

Q 116) H stands for________in HVAC systems.

1) Heating

2) Healing

3) Honning

4) Heavy

Q 117) ______________coil is fitted in HVAC system.

1) Both heating and cooling

2) Only heating

3) Only cooling

4) condensation

Q 118) In a car A.C., condenser is fitted near____________

1) radiator

2) rear wheel
3) crankcase
4) magnetic clutch

Q 119) Car A.C. operates at maximum efficiency when running at ________________

1) high speed
2) zero speed
3) low speed
4) zero load

Q 120) In order to____________ , dye is added to car A.C. system. ____________

1) identify the gas leak
2) lubricate the engine
3) increase efficiency
4) increase speed

Q 121) Which of the following does not affects heat load calculation in an A.C. plant

1) Outer temperature
2) Relative humidity
3) Dew point _
4) Moisture

Q 122) ______________in the condenser maintains the required level of water.

1) Flow switch
2) Overload circuit
3) Cut-out switch -
4) Strainer

Q 123) The application of fans and blowers in central A.C. plant is______________

1) circulation of air
2) heating
3) cooling
4) chilling

Q 124) The nature of air in summer air conditioning is____________

1) heated and humidified
2) heated and dehumidified
3) cooled and humidified
4) cooled and dehumidified

Q 125) If a deep freezer does not give enough cooling, then it must be due to_______________

1) continuous opening of door

2) no power supply

3) high external pressure

4) high external temperature

Q 126) Which of these is not a part of Ice cream plant

1) Ice bin

2) Heat exchanger

3) Pasteurizer

4) Homogenizer

Q 127) On switching on the _______________ , ice produced due to excess cooling starts melting

1) Defrost switch

2) Overload relay

3) Flow switch

4) Thermostat

Q 128) Carrot can be stored for 3 months at a temperature of ____________

1) 2 °C

2) 8 °C

3) 5 °C

4) 10 °C

Q 129) The unit of cold storage capacity is______.

1) tonne

2) kilogram

3) cubic metre

4) degree kelvin

61]In a refrigeration cycle, the flow of refrigerant is controlled by

(a)compressor

(b)condenser

(c)evaporator

(d)expansion valve

62]Where does the lowest temperature occur in a vapour compression cycle ?

(a) condenser

(b) evaporator

(c) compressor

(d)expansion valve

63]The leaks in a refrigeration system using Freon are detected by

(a)halide torch which on detection produces greenish flame lighting

(b)sulphur sticks which on detection gives white smoke

(c)using reagents

(d)smelling

64]rick up the incorrect statement

(a)lithium bromide used in vapour absorption cycle is nonvolatile

(b)lithium bromide plant can't operate below 0°C

(c)a separator is used in lithium bromide plant to remove the unwanted water vapour by condensing

(d)concentration of solution coming out of lithium bromide generator is more in comparison to that entering the generator

66]Mass flow ratio of NH3 in comparison to Freon12 for same refrigeration load and same temperature limits is of theorder of

(a)1 : 1

(b)1 : 9

(c)9 : 1

(d)1 : 3

67]Freon group of refrigerants are

(a)inflammable

(b)toxic

(c)noninflammable and toxic

(e)nontoxic and noninflammable]

68 Ammonia is

(a) nontoxic

(b) noninflammable

(c)toxic and noninflammable

(d)highly toxic and inflammable

69] In vapour compression cycle using NH3 as refrigerant, initial charge is filled at

(a)suction of compressor

(b)delivery of compressor

(c)high pressure side close to receiver

(d)low pressure side near receiver

70]Short horizontal lines on pressureenthalpy chart show

(a)constant pressure lines

(b)constant temperature lines

(c)constant total heat lines

(d)constant entropy lines

71] On the pressureenthalpy diagram, condensation and desuperheating is represented by a horizontal line because theprocess

(a)involves no change in volume

(b)takes place at constant temperature

(c)takes place at constant entropy

(e)takes place at constant pressure]

72]One ton of the refrigeration is

(a)the standard unit used in refrigeration problems

(b)the cooling effect produced by melting 1 ton of ice

(c)the refrigeration effect to freeze 1 ton of water at 0°C into ice at 0°C in 24 hours

(d)the refrigeration effect to produce 1 ton of ice at NTP conditions

73]Superheating in a refrigeration cycle

(a) increases COP

(b) decreases COP

(c)COP remains unaltered

(d)other factors decide COP

74]For proper refrigeration in a cabinet, if the temperature and vapour pressure difference between cabinet andatmosphere is high, then

(a) bigger cabinet should be used

(b)smaller cabinet should be used

(c)perfectly tight vapour seal should be used

(d)refrigerant with lower evaporation temperature should be used

75]Choose the correct statement

(a)A refrigerant should have low latent heat

(b)If operating temperature of system is low, then refrigerant with low boiling point should be used

(c)Precooling and subcooling bf refrigerant are same

(d)Superheat and sensible heat of a] refrigerant are same

76]The suction pipe diameter of refrigerating unit compressor in comparison to delivery side is

(a) bigger

(b) smaller

(c)equal

(d)smaller/bigger depending on capacity

77]Moisture in freon refrigeration system causes

(a)ineffective refrigeration

(b)high power consumption

(c)freezing automatic regulating valve

(d)corrosion of whole system

78]The advantage of dry compression is that

(a)it permits higher speeds to be used

(b)it permits complete evaporation in the evaporator

(c)it results in high volumetirc and mechanical efficiency

(d)all of the above

79]Choose the wrong statement

(a)Temperature of medium being cooled must be below that of the evaporator

(b)Refrigerant leaves the condenser as liquid

(c)All solar thermally operated absorption systems are capable only of intermittent operation

(d)frost on evaporator reduces heat transfer

80]Undercooling in a refrigeration cycle

(a) increases COP

(b) decreases COF

(c)COP remains unaltered

(d)other factors decide

81]For obtaining high COP, the pressure range of compressor should be

(a)high

(b)low

(c) optimum

(d)any value

(e) there is no such criterion]

82]The coefficient of performance is the ratio of the refrigerant effect to the

(a)heat of compression

(b)work done by compressor

(c)enthalpy increase in compressor

(d)all of the above

83]The C]O]P of a refrigeration cycle with increase in evaporator temperature, keeping condenser temperature constant,will

(a)increase

(b)decrease

(c)remain unaffected

(d)may increase or decrease depending on the type of refrigerant used

INDUSTRIAL TRAINING INSTITUTE

Monthly Test-1, Marks- 20, Date:- _______________

(Every Question Carry Two Marks)

Q 1) Which component creates flow of refrigerant in the system

1) Compressor

2) Evaporator

3) Condenser

4) Expansion valve

Q 2) A hermetically sealed compressor does not start when switched on and its motor does not hum. This could be due to ....

1) Faulty starting capacitor

2) Open - circuited motor windings

3) Low supply voltage

4) A seized up compressor _

Q 3) Thermo - compressor works on ....

1) Pascal s Law

2) Bernoulli s Principle

3) Dalton s Law

4) Avogadro s Law

Q 5) Which control provided in a refrigerator protects the compressor motor winding from damage

1) Starting relay

2) Overload protector

3) Thermostat

4) All of the above

Q 6) In absorption refrigeration system, the compressor of vapour compression system is replaced by ....

1) Absorber

2) Generator

3) Pump

4) All the above

Q 7) One of the desirable properties of refrigerant is that it should have ......

1) Low critical temperature

2) Low specific heat

3) Low thermal conductivity

4) Low electrical insulation

Q 8) Which of these refrigerants has the lowest Relative Ozone Destruction Efficiency

1) R - 11
2) R - 12
3) R - 22
4) R - 114

Q 9) A plate type evaporator is often used in a ....

1) Domestic air conditioner
2) Drinking water cooler
3) Domestic dehumidifier
4) Two-compartment refrigerator

Q 10) In a domestic refrigerator, the expansion valve used is ....

1) Capillary tube
2) Constant pressure expansion valve
3) Thermostatic expansion valve
4) Float valve

Q 23) The material used for production of fibreglass insulation is ....

1) Carbon
2) Pumice
3) Gypsum
4) Silica

INDUSTRIAL TRAINING INSTITUTE

Monthly Test-2, Marks- 20, Date:- ______________

(Every Question Carry Two Marks)

Q 21) The HFC refrigerant is ....

1) R11
2) R22
3) R134a
4) R290

Q 22) The capacity of a domestic refrigerator is approximately ....

1) 0.1 ton
2) O.5 ton
3) 1.0 ton
4) 1.5 ton

Q 23) The material used for production of fibreglass insulation is ....

1) Carbon
2) Pumice
3) Gypsum

4) Silica

Q 24) The insulating material which is NOT used in domestic refrigerator is .....

1) Wood fibre

2) Cork

3) Rubber

4) Glass wool

Q 25) Leakage in the refrigeration system using ammonia as refrigerant is detected by

1) Soap and water

2) Sulphur sticks

3) Halide torch

4) Burning candle

Q 26) What is the cause of refrigerant contamination

1) Moisture in refrigerant

2) Low oil level

3) High oil level

4) Short of gas

Q 27) The function of air diffuser in air conditioning is to ....

1) Clean air

2) Direct air flow in desired pattern

3) Reduce noise of air conditioner

4) Control relative humidity of air

Q 28) In flooded type of evaporator, expansion device used is ....

1) Non return valve

2) Float valve

3) Thermostatic device

4) Self-actuated expansion valve

Q 29) Which statement is NOT true about Vortex Tube (non conventional) refrigerating system

1) It uses air as refrigerant

2) It is light in weight

3) It requires less space

4) It has a number of moving parts

Q 30) Which of these is an example of application of Vortex Tube refrigerating system

1) Spot cooling of electronic components

2) Body cooling of workers in mines

3) Both of the above

4) None of the above

INDUSTRIAL TRAINING INSTITUTE

Monthly Test-3, Marks- 20, Date:- _______________

(Every Question Carry Two Marks)

Q 41) The heat rejection capacity of a condenser is affected by the following, except

1) Maximum pressure occuring at the condenser

2) Flow rate of cooling media in the condenser

3) Temperature difference between refrigerant and cooling media

4) Rate of flow of refrigerant in the condenser

Q 42) If the flow rate of refrigerant is high, which compressor will you choose

1) Reciprocating compressor

2) Centrifugal compressor

3) Screw compressor

4) Rotary compressor

Q 43) Performance of cooling tower is affected significantly by these factors, except .....

1) Approach

2) Wet bulb temperature

3) The range

4) TDS

Q 44) Inside cooling tower, a material is added to increase contact surface and contact time betwwen air and water. What is this material called

1) Insert

2) Pack

3) Fill

4) Core

Q 45) The disinfectants which can be used to get rid of viruses and bacteria are

1) Chlorine and water

2) Chlorine and ozone

3) Ultraviolet light and air

4) Ultraviolet light and water

Q 46) For small evaporators where refrigerant used is other than ammonia, tubing used is made of..

1) Steel

2) Copper

3) Brass

4) Bronze

Q 47) Why is it NOT recommended to clean condenser fins with a hose

1) Water will turn dirt into mud which will be hard to clean

2) Water will make the fins rust very quickly

3) Using hose is not bad. Recommendation need not be accepted

4) Using hose hardly does any damage to fins

Q 48) Why is it desirable for refrigerant entering the compressor to be slightly superheated

1) To prevent refrigerant oil from leaving the compressor

2) To prevent vapour refrigerant from entering the compressor

3) To keep compressor warm

4) To prevent liquid refrigerant from entering the compressor

Q 50) The purpose of HVAC system is to control ....

1) Temperature and humidity only

2) Supply of outside air

3) Air filtration and its movement in occupied spaces

4) All of the above

Q 52) As per heat load calculation, the load of AC II tier railway coach is about ....

1) 4 ton

2) 14 ton

3) 12 ton

4) 16 ton

INDUSTRIAL TRAINING INSTITUTE

Monthly Test-4, Marks- 20, Date:- _______________

(Every Question Carry Two Marks)

Q 61) ________________regulates the temperature inside the refrigeration cabinet.

1) Thermostat switch

2) Split phase motor

3) Relay

4) Overload protector

Q 63) Which of these capacity control methods of a compressor is also known as Cylinder unloader

1) Use of multiple units

2) Speed modulation

3) Hot gas bypass

4) ON OFF control

Q 65) The amount of water vapour present in a kilogram of dry air in the atmosphere is called __

1) specific humidity

2) air saturation

3) moist point

4) dry mass

Q 66) When the air is in saturated state, the value of wet bulb depression is________

1) zero

2) negative

3) maximum

4) unity

Q 67) To maintain human comfort, the value of air stratification should be kept __________

1) minimum

2) maximum

3) infinity

4) negative

Q 68) Which of the following facts is FALSE about Rigid Duct

1) Flexible

2) Expensive

3) Heavy

4) Water proof

Q 70) Sensible heat load is the product of sensible load, ___________and _____________

1) heat transmission factor, temperature

2) latent heat, temperature

3) temperature difference, mass

4) heat transmission factor, mass

1]Pick up the wrong statement] A refrigerant should have

(a)Tow specific heat of liquid

(b)high boiling point

(c)high latent heat of vaporisation

(d)higher critical temperature

Q 2) At constant pressure, volume varies as the temperature of the gas. This is statement of .....

1) Boyle s Law
2) Charles Law
3) Joule-Thompson Effect
4) Dalton s Law
Q 3) One ton of refrigeration = ...
1) 45.5 kcal min.
2) 50.4 kcal min.
3) 44.5 kcal min.
4) 66.5 kcal min

INDUSTRIAL TRAINING INSTITUTE

Monthly Test-5, Marks- 20, Date:- ______________

(Every Question Carry Two Marks)

2]A standard ice point temperature corresponds to the temperature of
(a)water at 0°C
(b)ice at 4°C
(c)solid and dry ice
(e)mixture of ice and water Under equilibrium conditions]
3]Vapour compression refrigeration is some what like
(a)Carnot cycle
(b)Rankine cycle
(c)reversed Camot cycle
(e)none of the above]
4]Which of the following cycles uses air as the refrigerant
(a)Ericsson
(b)Stirling
(c)Carnot
(d)Bellcoleman
5]Ammoniaabsorption refrigeration cycle requires
(a)very little work input
(b)maximum work input
(c)nearly same work input as for vapour compression cycle
(d)zero work input
6]An important characteristic of absorption system of refrigeration is
(a)noisy operation
(b)quiet operation
(c)cooling below 0°C
(d)very little power consumption
8]Clapeyron equation is a relation between

(a)temperature, pressure and enthalpy
(b)specific volume and enthalpy
(c)temperature and enthalpy
(e)temperature, pressure, specific volur and'enthalpy]
19]Clapeyron equation is applicable for registration at
(a)saturation point of vapour
(b)saturation point of liquid
(c)sublimation temperature
(d)triple point
(e)critical point]
10] In vapour compression cycle, the conditii of refrigerant is saturated liquid
(a)after passing through the condenser
(b)before passing through the condensei
(c)after passing through the expansion throttle valve
(d)before entering the expansion valve
11] In vapour compression cycle, the condition of refrigerant is very wet vapour
(a)after passing through the condenser
(b)before passing through the condenser
(c)after passing through the expansion or throttle valve
(e)before entering the compressor
12] In vapour compression cycle, the condition of refrigerant is high pressure saturated liquid
(a)after passing through the condenser
(b)before passing through the condenser
(c)after passing through the expansion or thiottle valve
(d)before entering the expansion valve

INDUSTRIAL TRAINING INSTITUTE

Monthly Test-6, Marks- 20, Date:- _______________

(Every Question Carry Two Marks)

Q 31) Temporary hardness of water is removed by ....
1) Filtering
2) Boiling
3) Chemical treatment
4) None of the above
Q 32) Natural draft cooling towers are mainly used in ....
1) Steel plants

2) Power stations
3) Fertilizer plants
4) Aluminium manufacturing plants

Q 33) What is used in pre-treatment of water to remove large objects
1) Bacteria
2) Oil and grease
3) Air
4) Screen

Q 34) In the evaporator the refrigerant enters at ....
1) Very low pressure
2) Low pressure
3) Medium pressure
4) High pressure

Q 35) The type of evaporator used in large refrigeration and central air conditioning systems is
1) Shell and tube evaporator
2) Finned evaporator
3) Plate surface evaporator
4) Bare tube evaporator

Q 36) Why are ice cans made tapered in height
1) To reduce weight
2) To facilitate dumping
3) To improve appearance
4) To make fabrication easier

Q 37) The instrument used to measure relative humidity is ....
1) Barometer
2) Psychrometer
3) Manometer
4) Pressure gauge

Q 38) Pressure on the high pressure side of a mechanical refrigeration unit is called
1) Suction pressure
2) Discharge or head pressure
3) Differential pressure
4) Absolute pressure

Q 42) Dry bulb temperature (DBT) is the actual temperature of ....
1) Moist air
2) Dry air

3) Dry ice

4) Saturated air

Q 43) AHU stands for ....

1) Air Handling Unit

2) Air Heating Unit

3) Air Humidifying Unit

4) None of these

INDUSTRIAL TRAINING INSTITUTE

Monthly Test-7, Marks- 20, Date:- _______________

(Every Question Carry Two Marks)

22]The condensing pressure due to the presence of noncondensable gases, as compared to that actually required forcondensing temperatures without noncondensable gases

(a) will be higher

(b) will be lower

(c)will remain unaffected

(d)may be higher or lower depending upon the nature of non-condensable gases

23]Critical pressure of a liquid is the pressure

(a)above which liquid will remain liquid

(b)above which liquid becomes gas

(c)above which liquid becomes vapour

(d)above which liquid becomes solid

24]Critical temperature is' the temperature above which

(a) a gas will never liquefy

(b) a gas will immediately liquefy

(c)water will evaporate

(d)water will never evaporate

25]The refrigerant for a refrigerator should have

(a) high sensible heat

(b) high total heatFluid

(c) high latent heat

(d)low latent heat

26]Rating of a domestic refrigerator is of the order of

(a)0]1 ton

(b) 5 tons

(c)10 tons

(d)40 tons

27]The COP of a domestic refrigerator
(a)is less than 1
(b)is more than 1
(c)is equal to 1
(d)depends upon the make
28]The domestic refrigerator uses following type of compressor
(a) centrifugal
(b)axial
(c)miniature sealed unit
(d)piston type reciprocating
29]Presence of moisture in a refrigerant affects the working of
(a) compressor
(b) condenser
(c) evaparator
(d) expansion valve]
30]Refrigeration in aeroplanes usually employs the following refrigerant
(a) Co2
(b)Freon11
(c) Freon22
(d)Air
31]Domestic refrigerator working on vapour compression cycle uses the following type of expansion device
(a)electrically operated throttling valve
(b)manually operated valve
(c)thermostatic valve
(d)capillary tube

INDUSTRIAL TRAINING INSTITUTE

Monthly Test-8, Marks- 20, Date:- ______________

(Every Question Carry Two Marks)

41]Absorption system normally uses the following refrigerant
(a) Freon11
(b) Freon22
(c) C02
(e) ammonia]
42] One of the purposes of subcooling the liquid refrigerant is to
(a)reduce compressor overheating
(b)reduce compressor discharge temperature
(c)increase cooling effect

(d)ensure that only liquid and not the vapour enters the expansion (throttling) valve

43] The value of COP in vapour compression cycle is usually

(a)always less than unity

(b)always more than unity

(c)equal to unity

(d)any one of the above

44] In a refrigeration system, heat absorbed in comparison to heat rejected is

(a) more

(b) less

(c)same

(d)more for small capacity and less for high capacity

45] Condensing temperature in a refrigerator is the temperature

(a)of cooling medium

(b)of freezing zone

(c)of evaporator

(d)at which refrigerant gas becomes liquid

46] Formation of frost on evaporator in refrigerator

(a)results in loss of heat due to poor heat transfer

(b)increases heat transfer rate

(c)is immaterial

(d)can be avoided by proper design

47] In refrigerators, the temperature difference between the evaporating refrigerant and the medium being cooled shouldbe

(a)high, of the order of 25°

(b)as low as possible (3 to 11°C)

(c)zero

(d)any value

48]In a flooded evaporator refrigerator, an accumulator at suction of compressor is used to

(a)collect liquid refrigerant and prevent it from going to compressor

(b)detect liquid in vapour

(c)superheat the vapour

(d)collect vapours

49]Accumulators should have adequate volume to store refrigerant charge at least

(a)10%

(b) 25%

(c) 50%

(d) 75%

50]At lower temperatures and pressures, the latent heat of vaporisation of a refrigerant

(a) decreases

(b)increases

(c)remains same

(d)depends on other factors

INDUSTRIAL TRAINING INSTITUTE

Monthly Test-9, Marks- 20, Date:- ______________

(Every Question Carry Two Marks)

51]A refrigeration cycle operates between condenser temperature of + 27°C and evaporator temperature of 23°C] TheCannot coefficient of performance of cycle will be

(a)0]2

(b)1]2

(c) 5

(d) 6

52]Which of the following is not a desirable property of a refrigerant

(a)high triiscibility with oil

(b)low boiling point

(c)good electrical conductor

(d)large latent heat

53]In vapour compression refrigeration system, refrigerant occurs as liquid between

(a)condenser and expansion valve

(b)compressor and evaporator

(c)expansion valve and evaporator

(d)compressor and condenser

54]Pick up the correct statement about giving up of heat from one medium to other in ammonia absorption system

(a)strong solution to weak solution

(b)weak solution to strong solution

(c)strong solution to ammonia vapour

(d)ammonia vapour to weak solution

55]Efficiency of a Cornot engine is given as 80%] If the cycle direction be reversed, what will be the value of COP ofreversed Carnot cycle

(a)1]25
(b)0]8
(c)0]5
(d) 0]25

56]Highest pressure encountered in a refrigeration system should be
(a)critical pressure of refrigerant
(b)much below critical pressure
(c)much above critical pressure
(d)near critical pressure

57] If a heat pump cycle operates between the condenser temperature of +27°C and evaporator temperature of 23°C,then the Carnot COP will be
(a)0]2
(b)1]2
(c) 5
(d)6

58]A certain refrigerating system has a normal operating suction pressure of 10 kg/cm gauge and condensing pressure ofabout 67 kg/cm] The refrigerant used is
(a)Ammonia
(b) Carbon dioxide
(c)Freon
(d) Brine

59]Aqua ammonia is used as refrigerant in the following type of refrigeration system
(a)compression
(b)direct
(c) indirect
(d) absorption

60]If the evaporator temperature of a plant is lowered, keeping the condenser temperature constant, the h]p] ofcompressor required will be
(a)same
(b) more
(c)less
(d)more/less depending on rating

INDUSTRIAL TRAINING INSTITUTE

Monthly Test-10, Marks- 20, Date:- ______________

(Every Question Carry Two Marks)

61]In a refrigeration cycle, the flow of refrigerant is controlled by (a)compressor

(b)condenser

(c)evaporator

(d)expansion valve

62]Where does the lowest temperature occur in a vapour compression cycle ?

(a) condenser

(b) evaporator

(c) compressor

(d)expansion valve

63]The leaks in a refrigeration system using Freon are detected by

(a)halide torch which on detection produces greenish flame lighting

(b)sulphur sticks which on detection gives white smoke

(c)using reagents

(d)smelling

64]rick up the incorrect statement

(a)lithium bromide used in vapour absorption cycle is nonvolatile

(b)lithium bromide plant can't operate below 0°C

(c)a separator is used in lithium bromide plant to remove the unwanted water vapour by condensing

(d)concentration of solution coming out of lithium bromide generator is more in comparison to that entering the generator

66]Mass flow ratio of NH3 in comparison to Freon12 for same refrigeration load and same temperature limits is of theorder of

(a)1 : 1

(b)1 : 9

(c)9 : 1

(d)1 : 3

67]Freon group of refrigerants are

(a)inflammable

(b)toxic

(c)noninflammable and toxic

(e)nontoxic and noninflammable]

68 Ammonia is

(a) nontoxic

(b) noninflammable

(c)toxic and noninflammable

(d)highly toxic and inflammable

69] In vapour compression cycle using NH3 as refrigerant, initial charge is filled at

(a)suction of compressor

(b)delivery of compressor

(c)high pressure side close to receiver

(d)low pressure side near receiver

70]Short horizontal lines on pressureenthalpy chart show

(a)constant pressure lines

(b)constant temperature lines

(c)constant total heat lines

(d)constant entropy lines

71] On the pressureenthalpy diagram, condensation and desuperheating is represented by a horizontal line because theprocess

(a)involves no change in volume

(b)takes place at constant temperature

(c)takes place at constant entropy

(e)takes place at constant pressure]

INDUSTRIAL TRAINING INSTITUTE

Monthly Test-11, Marks- 20, Date:- ______________

(Every Question Carry Two Marks)

72]One ton of the refrigeration is

(a)the standard unit used in refrigeration problems

(b)the cooling effect produced by melting 1 ton of ice

(c)the refrigeration effect to freeze 1 ton of water at 0°C into ice at 0°C in 24 hours

(d)the refrigeration effect to produce 1 ton of ice at NTP conditions

73]Superheating in a refrigeration cycle

(a) increases COP

(b) decreases COP

(c)COP remains unaltered

(d)other factors decide COP

74]For proper refrigeration in a cabinet, if the temperature and vapour pressure difference between cabinet andatmosphere is high, then

(a) bigger cabinet should be used

(b)smaller cabinet should be used

(c)perfectly tight vapour seal should be used

(d)refrigerant with lower evaporation temperature should be used

75]Choose the correct statement

(a)A refrigerant should have low latent heat

(b)If operating temperature of system is low, then refrigerant with low boiling point should be used

(c)Precooling and subcooling bf refrigerant are same

(d)Superheat and sensible heat of a] refrigerant are same

76]The suction pipe diameter of refrigerating unit compressor in comparison to delivery side is

(a) bigger

(b) smaller

(c)equal

(d)smaller/bigger depending on capacity

77]Moisture in freon refrigeration system causes

(a)ineffective refrigeration

(b)high power consumption

(c)freezing automatic regulating valve

(d)corrosion of whole system

78]The advantage of dry compression is that

(a)it permits higher speeds to be used

(b)it permits complete evaporation in the evaporator

(c)it results in high volumetirc and mechanical efficiency

(d)all of the above

79]Choose the wrong statement

(a)Temperature of medium being cooled must be below that of the evaporator

(b)Refrigerant leaves the condenser as liquid

(c)All solar thermally operated absorption systems are capable only of intermittent operation

(d)frost on evaporator reduces heat transfer

80]Undercooling in a refrigeration cycle

(a) increases COP

(b) decreases COF

(c)COP remains unaltered

(d)other factors decide

81]For obtaining high COP, the pressure range of compressor should be

(a)high

(b)low

(c) optimum

(d)any value

INDUSTRIAL TRAINING INSTITUTE

Monthly Test-12, Marks- 20, Date:- ______________

(Every Question Carry Two Marks)

Q 62) The efficiency of centrifugal compressors as compared to that of reciprocating compressors is

1) high

2) low

3) equal

4) low or equal

Q 63) Which of the following compressors are primarily considered as the most appropriate for refrigerant fluid

1) Scroll compressor

2) Hermetically sealed compressor

3) Swash plate compressor

4) Wobble plate compressor

Q 64) Wet compression____________the compressor efficiency.

1) increases

2) decreases

3) halves

4) has no effect on

Q 65) Water cooled condensers have ____________heat transfer rate as compared to air cooled condensers.

1) high

2) low

3) equal

4) low or equal

Q 66) Which of these is a tank shaped device used for storing liquid refrigerant in refrigeration

1) Liquid receiver

2) Condenser

3) Compressor oil charging pump

4) Evaporator

Q 67) The compressor compresses the refrigerant to high pressure to_____________

1) increase the temperature

2) heat the refrigerant

3) decrease the temperature

4) condense the refrigerant

Q 68) Both air and water are used as cooling medium in _________________ condenser.

1) evaporative
2) shell and tube
3) shell and coil
4) air cooled

Q 69) Plate surface evaporators are not used in____________

1) food processing industry
2) ice-cream cabinet -
3) domestic refrigerator
4) freezer

Q 70) In order to prevent the quantity of liquid refrigerant present in the refrigerant obtained from evaporator from entering into the condenser, ____________is connected between evaporator and compressor.

1) accumulator
2) superheater
3) bottle cooler
4) water cooler

Q 71) In reverse cycle defrosting, evaporator works like a_____________.

1) Condenser
2) evaporator itself
3) expansion valve
4) accumulator

9 798887 046297

Printed by Libri Plureos GmbH in Hamburg,
Germany